Media Literacy

Media Literacy

Seeking Honesty, Independence, and Productivity in Today's Mass Messages

Deidre Pike

International Debate Education Association

New York, London & Amsterdam

Published by
International Debate Education Association
P.O. Box 922
New York, NY 10009

This book is published with the generous support of the Open
Society Foundations.

Library of Congress Cataloging-in-Publication Data

Pike, Deidre M., 1965-
   Media literacy : seeking honesty, independence, and productivity in today's mass messages / Deidre Pike.
      pages cm
   ISBN 978-1-61770-085-9
   1. Media literacy--Study and teaching. I. Title.
   P96.M4P55 2014
   302.23--dc23

                                    2014008718

Design by Kathleen Hayes

Printed in the USA

◣ IDEBATE Press

Contents

Introduction: Media Stories on Which We Feed

"If you can control the storytelling, then you do not have to worry about who makes the laws."

—George Gerbner, media scholar and former dean of the Annenberg School[1]

Would you humiliate yourself in front of a huge television audience trying to win the affection of *The Bachelorette* or *The Bachelor* or singing off-key to gain media attention and possible fame? If you answered "maybe," you're not alone. Several thousand contestants show up for *American Idol* auditions every year in cities across the United States.[2] Many simply hope for a few minutes of television fame. Some dream of media superstardom.

OK, here is a harder question. Would you arm yourself with bow and arrow and battle to the death against a dozen other children for a reality television show? I sure hope your answer is "nope, nuh-uh, not ever." But maybe you are familiar with the concept, especially if you've read the best-selling book or watched the blockbuster movie *The Hunger Games*, a work of fiction set in a futuristic world where young people annually attempt to slaughter one another. How could a society end up not only tolerating but celebrating something like this? The popular novel explores how media forms can be used to shape and control how humans see our world and live in it.

The stories and messages told by contemporary mass media—from books to television to social media—are important tools in shaping a society. As media scholar George Gerbner noted above, if an entity—person, business or government—wields the power of media storytelling, that entity will also be molding and structuring other parts of the human experience, ultimately influencing even the lawmaking process.

Media Literacy is about understanding media messages on websites and social media feeds. It's about exploring the stories told in books, podcasts, magazines, cable sports networks, radio shows, parody news, and cartoons. Because media messages affect the way audiences view and engage with the real world, this book asks a few simple questions about media's honesty, independence from bias, and productivity in making the world a better place.

That's a tall order. Let's look at a couple of examples from both a contemporary book and a 100-year-old textbook.

The Hunger Games, a 2008 science fiction novel by Suzanne Collins, tells the story of a powerful and undemocratic government that controls the media. The government uses media messages, especially on television, to convince people that the only way their community can sustain its food supply is by cooperating with a gruesome reality TV show. The show pits children from various districts against one another in a bloody battle to the death. Who benefits from this dismal "game"? *The Hunger Games* depicts a Capitol of Panem where people enjoy ridiculous levels of wealth and comfort because of the hard work and inescapable poverty of all the other districts. Why don't people rebel in this fictional world? Because the government-controlled media persuade them that their experience of the world is better than any alternative.

Although it is a work of fiction, *The Hunger Games* offers an honest, independent, and productive glimpse into the consequences of media control, showing us how media stories can affect people's lives. Collins says she wrote about a fictional world to explore ideas that affect people in the real world. "Telling a story in a futuristic world gives you this freedom to explore things that bother you in contemporary times," she says. One problem that bothers her, she says, is "the power of television and how it's used to influence our lives."[3] Collins worries that young people, and even adults, aren't savvy enough about media to understand their emotions when watching, say, a reality TV show and coverage of real wars in countries like Afghanistan and Iraq. "There's this potential for desensitizing the audience so that when they see real tragedy playing out on the news, it doesn't have the impact it should," she says. "Because the young soldier's dying in the war in Iraq, it's not going to end at the commercial break. It's not something fabricated; it's not a game. It's your life."[4]

The Hunger Games is fiction, make-believe, a bad dream. In real life, in the United States, press freedom is protected from government control by the First Amendment to the U.S. Constitution.[5] But that doesn't mean media are exempt from any type of control. Factors that influence media in today's democracies include corporate ownership of media, pressures from audiences, demands of advertisers, and an unwillingness to challenge long-standing public attitudes about social values. These factors influence what we see, read, and hear in mass media today.

But mass media in the good old days of yesteryear weren't that much different.

College freshmen grimace when I read a 100-year-old textbook to them. In a McGuffey reader published in the late 1800s for kids in about the second grade, stories offer insights into family values and good citizenship. Stories feature polite children who listen to their parents. These obedient children appreciate nature. They are thankful for the wonderful things life offers. And they don't eat too much.

Wait—don't *eat* too much? Yes, that's the theme of a second-grade lesson called "The Greedy Girl," which I occasionally read aloud in my Introduction the Mass Communication class. The story focuses on Laura, a little girl who enjoys excessive quantities of food. "She isn't wise," the narrator adds, like the creatures of the forest who consume just enough and save extra, say, nuts for later. Gluttony has unpleasant consequences for Laura. The narrator concludes: "I do not love girls who eat too much. Do you, my little readers?"[6]

That's when my students groan and furrow their brows. Who does this McGuffey guy think he is? "I bet his wife and daughter end up with an eating disorder," one student suggests. We talk about why the author might have chosen this topic and this heavy-handed approach. We'd never see a children's story like this today, right? Then I hold up the latest edition of a woman's magazine with illustrations of impossibly thin women—made slimmer and more "perfect" by photo editing software. I ask students: "How much of a stretch from 'The Greedy Girl' to this?"

Good question. Today, some magazine editors talk a good line about empowering women of different sizes and shapes. An issue of *Cosmopolitan* magazine, for example, might contain an article about "out-of-whack" eating habits that don't qualify as anorexia or bulimia but are dangerous nonetheless. At the same time, the photographs in magazines like *Cosmopolitan* and *Vogue*—most often digitally altered to make women look slimmer and more "attractive"—seem to be saying the same thing as the narrator of "The Greedy Girl." Don't eat too much or people won't like you.

Savvy students understand that they're receiving mixed messages from contemporary mass media. This knowledge helps them navigate the flood of information they receive from TV, the Internet, print publications, and recorded music. That awareness is why *Media Literacy* exists.

What Are Media?

Everything we know that we didn't discover from direct contact with our environment, family, and friends, we learned from media. The word *medium*, the singular form of media, refers to a mode of communication that transmits information—words, sounds, images—from a maker to a receiver. If I'm walking in the forest and get too far ahead of my hiking partner, I might stop to lay out an arrow from sticks, put it at a fork in the road, and keep hiking. My partner arrives, sees the arrow, and knows which direction I took. In this case, the sticks are my medium—used to make a message for my partner. My partner knows how to read the message and uses the medium to make a decision.

A nightly network news broadcast on television is also a medium, one watched on an average evening by 22.5 million people in the United States.[7] So is a YouTube music video with 100 million hits or a social media status update viewed by 47 friends or followers. Media made for huge audiences are mass media, a category that includes television, websites, movies, books, newspapers, and radio shows. Because so many people encounter the messages of mass media, it's important to think about how they work and the role they play in our lives. Here are a few reasons why understanding mass media is important:

- Media stories shape our culture, serving both as a mirror of existing cultural practices and traditions and as a creator of new cultural traditions for audiences.[8]

- Media stories give us the perspectives and information needed to make good decisions about the paths we'll chose as we career through life.

- Media stories transport us into other worlds and give us a richer understanding of other people, places, and ways of thinking.

- Media stories hypnotize us, immersing us in a fantasy more interesting or preferable to our real lives.

- Media stories inspire us to imagine a better way of living in our worlds and act on our vision.

- Media stories help us form ideas that we carry into our real lives.

Media stories are powerful. Yet, we don't often give them much consideration. I've taught mass communication to college freshmen in Nevada, Hawai'i, and California. It still surprises me when college-aged adults say that they rarely or never think about the role of mass media in their lives. They watch television but don't consider its effect on their worldview or attitudes or actions. They listen to music without really hearing the lyrics or observing the style of the music. They watch advertising, lots of advertising, more advertising than at any previous time in the history of the human species. They're adults, so they know the point of advertising is to sell a product, service, or idea. But that doesn't mean they've given much thought to exactly how an advertisement works as a persuasive tool.

My goal is to help my students—and readers of this book—begin or continue the lifelong process of becoming media literate. I say "lifelong" because media literacy isn't a skill you acquire and then forget you've learned. It's perhaps one of the most important skills that you'll take with you as you launch out into the world of higher education, career, relationships, and family life. Your ability to analyze the media ranks as high as your studies in history, literature, and math. Media literacy will help you better navigate your academic experience, professional goals, and even your personal life.[9]

Media literacy is about exploring the stories told through media, reading them, listening carefully, and applying the skills of a media critic. For example, a media-literate person might watch a sporting event on television and consider what kinds of forces make her excited or bored during the show. During an election season, a media-literate person watches campaign commercials for political issues and works to understand what persuasive tools are being used to convince audiences to believe or vote a certain way.

Media literacy helps humans have a conversation about who and what the media are representing and why many media messages represent these subjects the way they do. Two student athletes once showed my class clips from the reality TV show *Basketball Wives* and started a class discussion about how this show portrays race. Does the show rely on racial stereotypes to entertain its audience?[10]

A media-literate individual isn't quick to judge a specific medium as terrific or trashy. Media-literacy educators note that it's not always *what* you watch or listen to or read but *how* you watch, listen to, and read media. A media-literate individual knows how to be a critic, asking good questions about media. She's not a cheerleader, clapping her hands over every exciting new media trend. And she's not a cynic, automatically assuming the worst and wagging a finger.

Finally, media literacy can encourage you to use your own voice, giving you ideas about how to construct your own messages and how to use your media-making powers responsibly. A media-literate person might start a social media discussion about race or gender in Disney cartoons, create a YouTube playlist of music that promotes social justice, or write a blog about popular video games. Media literacy, it turns out, is contagious.

A Memorable Acronym for Media Critics

The goal of this book is to raise awareness of a variety of issues in all types of media—from social networks to blogs to YouTube videos to sports coverage and even to video games and cartoons. That's a big task. How could we chop something as large as this up into manageable, bite-sized chunks? That's the question I had in mind when I started to plan this project. I decided that what I needed was a simple and memorable acronym that could be applied to all media to look at them critically.

I tried to come up with three simple attributes or qualities that a person could look for in a particular medium or a media genre, like parody news. I chose three values I care about—truth, bias, and usefulness. As an acronym, that turned out to be TBU. I wasn't excited.

Besides the bad acronym, some of the terms were problematic. *Truth* is a difficult word to define. A novel like *The Hunger Games* or the latest movie in *The Lord of the Rings* series can be not exactly truthful but still seem meaningful. Although the stories are fabricated, a character may encounter a problem or situation that seems familiar to me—something to which I can relate. When fiction resembles my own experience so much that I identify with the characters or situation, it seems—honest.

The word *bias* was also a problem because it describes a medium that's slanted or shaped to promote one idea while excluding another. That's not something you want in media. A much better value might be described as independence, an open medium that doesn't lean too far in one direction.

And what exactly does the word *useful* mean? The word seems limp and passive. I decided that *productive* might be a better word and a better way to think about usefulness. I am a useful person, most days. I have some skills that can be employed to do lots of things. But some days I am more productive than others, putting my potential into action. That seems an important value for media as well.

So my new acronym was born. What if we asked about the honesty of a medium, questioned its independence, and gauged its productivity? That's an easier acronym because it spells out a word—HIP.

HIP?

Sorry, but that's not very "hip," as in trendy, fashionable, and current. I explained my plan to a friend who was working on a doctoral degree in literature at the University of California, Berkeley. Her school has always seemed like a hip place to me. My friend was politely opposed to my plan, arguing that it's *not* hip to use HIP as a media acronym. Her boyfriend, a lawyer in San Francisco, agreed. We spent some time trying to come up with something better.

> Honesty, openness, productivity—HOP.
>
> Honesty, accuracy, productivity—HAP.
>
> Honesty, independence, handiness—HIH.

In the end, I liked HIP the best. It seems the easiest to remember. So, in this book, we'll talk about the qualities of honesty, independence, and productivity in the hopes of finding out what media work the best in our own media diets.

In the following chapters, we'll see how these three values overlap, how honesty and independence are closely linked—and yet even an honest and independent medium can be unproductive. I like examples, so I'll use lots of them.

A "Dangerous" Tool!

In 1999, author and media critic Douglas Rushkoff noted that the United States was the only developed nation in the world that didn't make media literacy a required part of its public school curriculum. "Media literacy is dangerous," he writes in his book *Coercion: Why We Listen to What "They" Say*.[11] "Not to the individuals who gain it but to the people and institutions that depend on our *not* having it."

Here's why.

Once you're armed with the tools of a media critic, you use them—on every single bit of media from a 30-second commercial to the Netflix series on which you're binging to a cable news show that picks apart a lawmaker's speech. "If we learn the techniques that an advertiser uses to fool us, we have also learned the techniques that a government uses," Rushkoff writes.[12]

Does that mean becoming a conspiracy theorist? Looking for hidden agendas in every bit of media that comes our way? Rushkoff warns that it's tempting to think of some large organized force that we can label "they," as in it's "us" against "them." But that can lead to cynicism, the dark side of media literacy. The advertising executive is not a bad person involved in some large conspiracy to brainwash the public. Neither is the public relations agency hired to repair a celebrity's image after she's been caught shoplifting. The celebrity herself isn't part of the conspiracy any more than you, watching at home, clicking on the latest online gossip and recommending it to social network friends. We're all in this together.

Optimistic, forward-thinking media criticism can break the cycle for everyone. We can all become more aware as media consumers, more mindful of the messages we ingest, more critical of their value in our lives and their impact on our worldviews. If media consumers demand work that's honest, independent, and productive, media makers will respond to this demand.

Recently, I went to hear Canadian author Naomi Klein talk about the content of a book and documentary film she was working on.[13] In Klein's writing and visual media, she wants to deliver a message of hope—hope that people will realize the urgency of global climate change and work together to craft a more sustainable way of living. One of the reasons that people don't do this, she suggested, is because we think humans are supposed to be selfish and greedy. We think that humans are supposed to be selfish and greedy because that's a message foisted on us by media—from reality television to sports to news coverage of the banking industry. We have been "programmed" by the programs we watch.

We don't have to believe these messages. Critical viewers can figure out how to avoid being "programmed." As aware media consumers, we can learn to see through the stories we're told by mass media. As thoughtful media producers, we can make new messages. We can become the shapers of our own future and the future of our species.

Does this sound overwhelming? To be honest, yes, it does. Rushkoff writes that we are so used to the media's messages, to their coercive programming, that we may feel "powerless, passive, or depressed . . . suspicious and cynical."[14] That feeling, however, is another effect of the mass media, one that you can overcome. You don't have to feel helpless. You have power—over yourself, your media consumption, your view of the world. You have options and ways of taking action. You can become a critic—a person who looks carefully at examples of media and evaluates them knowledgeably—instead of a cynic who becomes angry and dismisses all media as lies and more lies.

The key is to not give up. In her talk, Klein told those of us in a crowded California university auditorium that it's a great time to be alive. We have so many choices about what to do with our time and energy. We can learn to make good choices, not just for us but for the humans who will inherit the blissful future we create. That's the passion that fuels the media critic.

1 Care and Feeding of Mediated Me

"The better part of my work on media is actually somewhat like a safe-cracker's. I don't know what's inside. Maybe it's nothing. I just sit down and start to work. I grope, I listen, I test, I accept and discard. I try out different sequences—until the tumblers fall and the doors spring open."

—Marshall McLuhan, *Understanding Media*[1]

In the United States, people take in about 12 hours of mediated information every day outside of their schools and workplaces.[2] That includes time spent watching television, reading books and magazines, listening to radio or prerecorded music, surfing the Internet, talking on phones, playing video games, and going to the movies.[3]

In all, U.S. media users consumed 3.6 zettabytes of information during one year, according to a study by the Global Information Industry Center at the University of California, San Diego.[4] How much info is that? The study authors describe it like this: If 3.6 zettabytes were printed as text in books and piled across every inch of the United States, including Alaska, the pile would be seven feet deep. Seven feet. We're over our heads in content—buried, in fact.

How do we sort through all this information, make sense of it, and find the good stuff, the info we need to make good decisions about our lives and our worlds? Good question. Media-literacy tools help us understand and exert some control over the media we consume—and over contributions we make to the info landscape of others.

Media critics work like nutritionists, looking at the food you eat and suggesting better choices. A media critic explores ingredients used in our entertainment and information "meals." We're always at work, seeking balanced info snacks for contemporary times. Learning to think like a media critic compels us to think about our consumption choices, learning to balance media junk food with nutritious content. Perhaps you know the saying—"You are what you eat." The saying applies to media content as easily as it does to a balanced diet.

Media critics head for the buffet table of information and entertainment with an open mind. The lines between information (documentaries, news, reference websites) and entertainment (music, video games, reality TV) aren't always distinct. A news program intended as informational might address a shallow issue (pet fashion shows!) that's about as nutritious as a Pop-tart. In contrast, the entertaining 20-minute cartoon may get dismissed as meaningless cheesy puffs. But a closer look reveals that this animation makes you think twice about an important issue you'd never before considered.

A student of media can't be too quick to judge between "good" or highbrow media and "bad" mindless junk without spending some time observing the medium and asking three questions:

- Is the medium honest—resembling reality fairly?

- Is the medium independent—free from bias?

- Is the medium productive—with the potential to make the world a better place?

A nutritious media diet contains information and entertainment sources that are all of the above—honest, independent, and productive. As an acronym, that's HIP. Although the *Urban Dictionary* defines *hip* as "cooler than cool, the pinnacle of what is 'it,'" clearly the word becomes less "cool" when used as a media literacy acronym.

Few media combine a satisfactory mix of honesty, independence, and productivity. Some media content might be honest but barely independent and not at all productive. Like celebrity gossip. But the media critic keeps an open mind. Could there be a productive side to knowing the latest about a celebrity's baby daddy? Does our fascination with the lives of the famous contribute to our society? The critic avoids cynicism and doesn't jump to conclusions. She spends some time gathering evidence about the honesty, independence, and productivity of Miley Cyrus news reports before concluding that they're unHIP.

Feeding on Media

We consume foods and beverages to fuel our bodies. Food can be examined for its calorie content, its percentage of fat and sugar, and its other nutrients from carbohydrates to protein, fiber, iron, and vitamins. A person with minimal knowledge of nutrition knows that some foods are better fuel for the human body than others. We consume media content to fuel our minds, attitudes, and actions—and also for entertainment and distraction. Like food, media content can be examined to discover its nutrients.

Many systems exist for evaluating media content. For example, media education professor David Buckingham explores the media influence on children by looking at media technologies, economics, texts, and audiences. Buckingham asks how media technologies have changed to make more information available and easy to access. He looks at how a TV cartoon, today, becomes a merchandising bonanza with branded clothing, lunch boxes, stickers, food and "a myriad of other products."[5] He discusses how commercial media expose inequalities between the rich and poor who "live not just in different social worlds, but in different media worlds as well."[6]

Handy modes for critiquing media often vary depending on what medium is under the magnifying glass. A critic of news media might evaluate a newspaper or journalistic broadcast looking for how the journalists report, verify, and publish information. Those are elements of news literacy. The news-literate human, then, watches cable news or reads an editorial in the *Washington Post* looking for accurate information that's been fact-checked and verified, that's independent of bias, and for which some source is accountable.

Our experiences with media today, of course, extend well beyond the realm of news media. Even in a university class, few students say they get information from traditional sources like newspapers or broadcast journalism. We might, instead, be gleaning stories and information from a comedy news show, from reality television, documentaries, social media—even video games. The HIP factor can be examined in all of these media sources—from social networks to recorded music.

In looking at media examples, we begin with the understanding that the stories we are told make a difference in how we experience our worlds—whether these stories are being told by a CBS news reporter or J. K. Rowling in a Harry Potter book. In defining media, theorist Walter Lippmann observed that humans adjust to our environments through fictions. He didn't use the word *fiction* the way we do in English class today, describing vampire novels like *Twilight*. To Lippmann, a "fiction" meant any representation (CNN news story or Disney cartoon) that humans make to explain ourselves and our worlds. A "fiction," he theorized, was any form of media that selects, rearranges, and presents the "ebb and flow of [direct] sensation."[7]

Sound complicated? Here's another way to look at media: a medical definition describes media as an "intervening substance" through which "something else is transmitted."[8] Our entertainment, information, and news media intervene between humans and the gigantic real world. Media transmit this real world to us by breaking off bits and pieces and condensing these into a YouTube video, a Facebook post, or a story in daily newspaper. "[T]he real environment is altogether too big, too complex, and too fleeting for direct acquaintance," Lippmann suggested. "To traverse the world, [people] must have maps of the world."[9] Take a minute to wrap your brain around that.

Our media, then, are our maps of the real world. But who are our mapmakers? So glad you asked. Lippmann believed that the public needed educated elites to create maps that would shape our experiences. Psychologist and education reformer John Dewey disagreed. Dewey thought that people could be educated, taught to discern fact from fiction, and could become critically thinking citizens. He saw the danger in relying on an elite mapmakers alone— no matter how pure their intentions—to tell our stories for us. These days, with access to social media, the ability to upload our own videos and build our own blogs and websites, we have more mapmaking abilities in our own hands. Becoming a mapmaker and developing the habits of a media critic are Dewey-like projects for those who believe that humans are educable. If our schools haven't yet given us useful media-literacy skills, we can take the responsibility into our own hands. That's the purpose of this book.

To return to our food metaphor, just as few "superfoods" exist that offer ideal nutrients for human bodies, few "supermedia" exist that would earn perfect scores on all three attributes of honesty, independence, and productivity. Most media examples will land on a sliding scale between those that are socially healthful and intellectually nutritious to others that contain enough brain sugar to provoke diabetes of the neurons. That's why media diversity is important. We should have plenty of media choices at the buffet of information and entertainment.

But wait. Maybe I don't want to be media literate, you say. What if I have to give up something I like? Even a savvy media critic might not choose to eliminate media junk from our diets entirely. That'd be like living on the media equivalent of broccoli and gluten-free bread. A delicious piece of chocolate can be part of a balanced diet just as a clever meme or TV sitcom can accompany a balanced menu of useful and informative media.

Don't worry. You aren't going to starve.

Media Honesty

When we watch a blockbuster movie like *Avatar* (2009), we know the setting, story, and characters are science fiction. The movie's action unfolds on Pandora, obviously not a real planet, and the character mix includes fantastically tall blue humanoids whose long braids of hair plug into the natural and spiritual world. It's obvious that *Avatar* is fantasy, augmented by our 3-D glasses. So it's not a truthful medium overall—it's fiction.

That said, the movie's theme is one to which we can relate—a community coming together to fight greed and exploitation. The conflict may even resemble events happening in the news. For example, mining for "unobtainium" on the fictional planet Pandora could correlate, in real life, to drilling for oil in Alaska's pristine wilderness. How are conflicts resolved in *Avatar*? A hero brandishing spectacular weapons emerges to save the day. That's Hollywood's solution to many problems and we like it. But not all real-life problems are solved by hero intervention. The extent to which the movie's resolution mirrors reality might offer an honest glimpse of how the world works. Or we might find a movie's happy endings to be as fake as the floating islands of Pandora.

We may have higher expectations for honesty in nonfiction media, like news programs. When we watch lawmakers and other public figures speak on a cable news show, we expect the content of the speech to resemble reality much more closely than a Hollywood movie. We expect truth. When lawmakers' words don't match their actions or when verifiable facts emerge that conflict with what's been said, we accuse the speakers of lying.

In a culture that values honesty, misrepresentations provoke anger and cynicism. Some familiar historic examples: Pres. Bill Clinton says of White House intern Monica Lewinsky, "I did not have sex with that woman." Evidence piles up suggesting that Clinton had sex with Lewinsky. Years later, to justify invading Iraq, Pres. George W. Bush says the U.S. military is certain that Iraq has weapons of mass destruction (WMD). But the "facts" he cites turn out to be fictions. No WMDs ever turn up in Iraq. Given these examples, we might find it hard to know who or what to believe.

Humans crave accurate information to help us understand our world. We are hungry for news of people, events, and issues outside our direct experience. Experts in journalism call this the "awareness instinct" and suggest that news media's first obligation is "to the truth."[10] Authors Bill Kovach and Tom Rosenstiel write in *The Elements of Journalism*: "[T]he purpose of journalism is to provide people with the information they need to be free and self-governing."[11] That's a high calling and a huge responsibility. Finding accurate information and verifying its truth—how closely it resembles reality—is foundational to the democratic practices of a country like the United States.

This responsibility to mirror reality should extend to all forms of media, even the fictions of TV situation comedies or radio talk shows. We should seek honesty in all forms of information and entertainment media. This helps us find the media that influence our decisions about how to live and participate in society. What kinds of questions might we ask? We'll show plenty of examples in the rest of this book, but here are a few stories to explore for their honesty:

- Is mining an irredeemably evil villainous industry, as depicted in the movies *Avatar* and *Ferngully*?

- How does Kanye West's lyrical assertion of the worth of a "good girl" in his song "Bound 2" hold up given that the song's music video features a topless reality TV star?

- Does a man's dandruff cause women to evaporate, as suggested by the advertisers of Axe Anti-Dandruff shampoo?

Media mapmakers create images of our world and how it works. These maps need to be examined and reexamined for their honesty. Examples of honest media might be found in online newspapers, recorded music, movies—and even comedy shows on cable TV. A newspaper or broadcast news program that seeks to be known as truthful, for example, may run corrections that admit and correct errors of fact. A popular prime-time cartoon depicts a dysfunctional family to which thousands of fans relate. A company takes responsibility for its environmental problems. That's honest.

These days, we're making more of our own maps. Honesty becomes an important value for us to seek in making media, whether a 140-character microblog post or a streaming video that may go viral. Are we helping create a clear version of reality? Or are we blurring the images on the map?

The media critic observes media sources carefully to answer the above questions. We might find some media that offer muddled messages or even blatant lies. We'll find other media to be honest and clear. We can make these nutritious media sources part of our balanced media diet.

Media Independence

In 2001, not long after hijacked planes flew into the World Trade Center, political satirist Bill Maher made controversial comments on his show *Politically Incorrect.* Maher was responding to Pres. George W. Bush's suggestion that suicidal terrorists were "cowards." Maher replied: "We have been the cowards, lobbing cruise missiles from 2,000 miles away: That's cowardly. Staying in the airplane when it hits the building, say what you want about it, it's not cowardly." His words struck a nerve. Some felt Maher had stepped over the line, insulting U.S. military forces.

Since the show was called *Politically Incorrect,* you might think viewers would understand that Maher's stock-in-trade was brutal honesty. Not the case. Maher had seemed unpatriotic. Sears and Federal Express pulled advertising from the show. Seventeen stations dropped his program. To mitigate the damage, Maher apologized. But his apology was too little, too late. It didn't placate the angry masses. And it alienated those who felt that Maher had made an important, brave statement. "Maher should resign, not for what he said but for flying under false colors," complained *The Nation* columnist Victor Nabosky. "You can't have a show called *Politically Incorrect* and then abjectly apologize for not being PC."[12] In the end, Maher's show was canceled.

But wait, you ask, what about freedom of speech and the press? Doesn't Maher have a constitutional right to his views, even if they are controversial? In the United States, the First Amendment to the U.S. Constitution guarantees that the U.S. government cannot make laws that infringe on our rights to free speech and a free press.

Here's the complication. It's one thing to be exempt from government control. It's another for mass media to be free of corporate control, the influence of advertisers, and concerns about offending audiences. Media are businesses. The goal of, say, Disney-owned ABC television and news networks is to make a profit for the company and its stockholders. Understanding media as for-profit businesses is key to understanding media content in the United States and similar nations.

In the twentieth century, as broadcast media technologies like radio and television emerged, governments around the world made decisions about how this potent new information source might be used. In some countries, governments decided to strictly control content. The programming offered would entertain and inform audiences, while working to instill proper, government-approved values and behaviors.

This high level of control—foisting a government's point of view on all media audiences—may sound outrageous to those in countries, the United States among them, with media sources that operate largely independent of government censorship. In George Orwell's novel *1984*, government-controlled mass media continually rewrite history. All information was intended to foster an attitude or spark a behavior approved by leaders and lawmakers. If the leaders changed, entire volumes of history would be rewritten so that opposing voices never existed, never held positions of power. That's scary.

In the United States, media companies are most often private businesses with some government regulation. The Federal Communications Commission regulates broadcast media content moderately, forbidding offensive language and some vulgar themes from being broadcast on the public's airwaves. The agency also controls ownership by handing out (or taking away) licenses for broadcast media and making rules about how many TV or radio stations a company can own. The goal of regulation is information diversity—having many media companies offering an array of media from varied perspectives. From time to time in U.S. media history, when a media monopoly seemed to threaten information diversity, the federal government has stepped in to regulate the market, to keep things fair. Other than that, for decades, media companies have been free to create programming that people wanted. People had choices—and this served democracy well.

Some recent trends have shifted this balance of media power. Laws that ensured information diversity, that kept media companies smaller and more competitive, had eroded by the 1990s. An era of deregulation—less government oversight of ownership and fairness issues—allowed media companies to merge and grow exponentially. Today, most U.S. media sources are owned by a handful of global media corporations run by boards of directors and highly paid executives.[13] People who invest in these large companies expect them to make a profit.

While the U.S. Constitution guarantees media freedom from government control, corporate ownership fosters a different value system—one that might lead to media self-censorship. Employees of a media company may end up having to choose between publishing or broadcasting a truthful message or pleasing advertisers and audiences with tamer, less controversial content. While it's easy to spot Orwellian propaganda in a government-controlled media, the manipulation of a for-profit press is harder to identify.

To see how corporate ownership influences media content, we'll start by thinking about how for-profit media make money directly from media consumers and from advertisers that pay to promote a product, person, or service. First, profits can come directly from audiences, as in the case of people who shell out $18 to see *The Lorax* in 3-D or buy Rihanna's latest album at Target. Some companies, like an Internet connection, mobile phone service, cable TV, or Netflix subscriptions, sell access to media. Second, media companies make a profit by selling air time to advertisers. A 30-second commercial during the Super Bowl cost $1.5 million in 2012. The Super Bowl commands that kind of money because it's the most-watched television program in the United States.

Because of the profit that comes from both their audience and their advertisers, media companies may be more motivated to produce content that is uncontroversial and that has the widest possible appeal. Controversy is risky. It might annoy audiences or frighten advertisers. Think back to the example of Bill Maher's assertions on *Politically Incorrect*. Advertisers were afraid to be associated with Maher's incendiary comments. Money was lost. Media makers think long and hard before disseminating content that would offend advertisers.

Some content seems crafted expressly to attract advertisers, like home and personal makeover TV shows. No longer content with 60-second commercials, advertisers now pay for product placement or brand integration within a program's content. When a reality TV show participant drinks a major cola brand in front of 20 million viewers, that paid advertising is part of the show. Since those viewers are a product that the show's owners sell to advertisers, keeping an audience tuned in is the key to success.

Media makers study audiences to see what entertains people the most—what holds their attention. Few media sources overtly challenge the long-held beliefs and traditions of mass audiences. This storytelling filter is an ideological one that keeps less popular ideas out of the public eye. Media critic Marshall McLuhan described "acceptable entertainment" as media that "flatters" what a culture already believes about itself.[14] A TV show that doesn't make a nation feel good about its citizens and its freedoms, for example, would not likely be a success.

In their book, *Manufacturing Consent: The Political Economy of the Mass Media*, Edward Herman and Noam Chomsky describe several forces that filter what we see and hear on our screens and the airwaves. These filters include demands of advertisers and the owners of media companies. "Dominant media firms are quite large businesses . . . controlled by wealthy people or by managers who are subject to sharp constraints by owners . . . and have important common interests with other major corporations, banks, and government," Herman and Chomsky write.[15] The authors make a case that these monied elites use media to placate the working class and to discourage folks from working for social change through organized action.

American journalist A. J. Liebling once described the dilemma for independent media in his famous remark: "Freedom of the press is guaranteed only to those who own one." Media companies are businesses. In a nation like the United States, money dictates the bias of for-profit media far more than liberal or conservative politics. Entertainment and news media are both in danger of pandering to corporate owners, advertisers, and audiences. The media critic evaluates media sources and seeks those that may be more independent than others, those that offer free and uncensored expression.

Media Productivity

"Make money" may be the operating motto for contemporary mass media but a more socially progressive motto might be derived from Jonas Salk's famous quote: "Our greatest responsibility is to be good ancestors."[16] Media productivity, for the purposes of this book, measures how much mass media improve the world, helping today's audiences become "better ancestors."

Better ancestors are humans who consider both future generations and other living beings that share this lovely whirling dirtball we call home. Our own better ancestors fought for free speech, rights for women and minorities, and class equality. Some were innovative, crafting things that made our lives easier, like the Internet and indoor plumbing. Salk lived his motto, developing a vaccine that helped to nearly eliminate polio around the globe.

How can we charge mass media with such a gigantic responsibility? Shouldn't our values come from our families, our churches, our social circles, and our schools? Of course, all these help people create a baseline of sturdy values. At the same time, we spend much of our time exposed to mediated messages about our environments. These messages alter our baseline, evoke various emotions, shift perspectives, and will even cause us to act differently. If a song makes you sad or a hamburger commercial makes you crave French fries, that's a media effect. If you change your mind about a presidential candidate after watching a televised debate, that's a media effect. "Media effects are happening all around us every day," writes W. James Potter in *Media Literacy*. "And those effects are not just happening to other people; they are happening to all people."[17]

Media shape our culture. Our idea of the American Dream, the certainty that a person can become successful, famous, or wealthy if she tries hard enough, can be traced back to Horatio Alger[18] novels. This rags-to-riches myth repeats itself in TV shows, movies, and even news media that are drawn to stories of success.

A media critic spends time examining the usefulness of media messages that affect our understanding of reality. People who watch more television are more likely to believe that the world is a dangerous, scary place because of the amount of crime in TV entertainment and in news media. Researcher George Gerbner observed TV watchers and theorized the "Mean World Syndrome." He suggested that viewers who watch more than three hours of TV per day are exposed to so much media violence that they believe the world is "meaner" than those who watch less TV.[19] The TV content problem isn't confined to hour-long cop dramas, but also extends to news media content. "If it bleeds, it leads" sums up the wry mantra of much TV news in the United States.

Gerbner suggests the most "debilitating" consequence of the Mean World Syndrome involves its impact on our actions. His research showed that the more television people watch, the more they stay home, especially at night. "They are afraid of strangers and meeting other people," he wrote. "A hallmark of civilization, which is kindness to strangers, has been lost."[20]

Can a media critic find examples of the opposite effect—call it the "Kind World Syndrome"? Sure—and that's where media can be most productive. The fictional and real characters in our media stories may become models for our own behavior. The animated cast of the *Toy Story* trilogy models loyal friendships. *Modern Family* teaches us that families today may look different but loving bonds between caring partners, parents, and children remain the same. When news media record footage of Michelle Obama planting her White House garden, we see the value of growing our own produce, making steps toward living sustainably.

The question of productivity overlaps with previous discussions of honesty and independence. Can the media's impact on human thinking and behavior be sold to the highest bidder through advertising and public relations? That's a question with which media critics grapple.

Gerbner calls for "a more diverse, more fair, more sane, more equitable cultural environment."[21] Today's media critic must look beyond message manipulation to seek media that make their audiences better ancestors. Media critics place a high value on media that have a strong positive impact on individual emotions, attitudes, and actions and also, in a larger sense, a beneficial effect on local, national, and global communities. Messages that do this could be considered useful, productive media content. Examples of productive media are numerous:

- Former vice president Al Gore narrates a feature-length documentary movie, *An Inconvenient Truth*, to educate a wide audience about global warming and the national conversation shifts. A dialogue begins as we debate how to best mitigate greenhouse gasses and forestall the dire consequences of climate change.

- Google executive Wael Ghonim creates a Facebook group that helps to inspire a youth revolution in Egypt.

- A San Diego nonprofit group, Invisible Children, creates a moving 30-minute documentary about central African warlord Joseph Kony; the YouTube video goes viral, with tens of millions of viewers in the first week. Although questions eventually emerge about the video, its maker, and the organization, the U.S. government increases its efforts to apprehend Kony.

At this point, it's evident that the three components of the HIP factor are interdependent. Media that are productive—that make us better ancestors—are also likely to be honest and independent.

BE THE CRITIC

Observe and evaluate your own media consumption. How balanced is your diet of TV shows, video games, music, mobile devices, and social networks?

- Record your media use on a typical day. Write down every bit of media you consume from the music that you listen to while brushing your teeth to the billboards you walk past on the way to school. Include content you access on your cell phone. Include the time of day and any other relevant details, like your location, your companions, and even your mood.

- Look for patterns in your media consumption. How often do you check your social network sites? At what time of day? Are you alone or with friends, family?

- Think about what those patterns mean. Do you watch a particular TV show with friends as a social event? Do you check your Facebook page more often if you're alone?

- Evaluate your media diet. Does everything seem balanced? Are you consuming more than you thought? Does anything need to change?

- Finally, write a media action plan for yourself. If you've decided that your media consumption levels are fine, write them out as a guide for future reference. If something needs to change, write some media goals for yourself, things you'd like to improve. *Voilà!* You're gaining critical skills.

SATIATE YOUR CURIOSITY

- How much information comes at American consumers each year? Who makes it? How does the United States compare globally? Keep track of the latest info and research at the Global Information Industry Center website at the University of California, San Diego. http://hmi.ucsd.edu/howmuchinfo.php

- Watch the AMC series *Mad Men*, a drama set in a 1960s advertising agency in New York City. The show's entertaining and smart, and it gives its audience a crash course in media literacy.

- Look for "KONY 2012," a video and campaign by Invisible Children that pushes for the arrest of notorious African warlord Joseph Kony. The 30-minute documentary is on YouTube and various other video sites online.

2 Print Media

"[Journalists] hate being lied to. They hate it because it is wrong. They hate it because it thwarts the purposes of a free press. And they hate it because it makes them look bad to publish something that later turns out not to be right."

—Charles Lane, editor of *The New Republic*

James Frey's popular memoir, *A Million Little Pieces,* kept talk show host Oprah Winfrey up all night. His 2003 book described his true-life tales of drug addiction, run-ins with cops, jail time, and recovery. Winfrey's endorsement of Frey's book catapulted its sales. Around 1.7 million copies of the book, published by HarperCollins,[1] were sold in 2005. The only book that outsold Frey that year was *Harry Potter and The Goblet of Fire.*

The memoir was supposed to be nonfiction—Frey's authentic, real, lived experience. But the author's facts did not check out. Frey's make-believe adventures were exposed by the Smoking Gun website, a site that publishes legal documents and arrest records. The website's staff had tried to find a simple mug shot of Frey from one of his many arrests. What they eventually found was a dismal lack of evidence that the author's claims were true.[2] Frey had embellished some truths—and invented others. Much of his memoir was, in fact, fiction. That wouldn't be a problem if the book had been labeled a novel. But Frey had claimed his memoir was a true story. He lied.

Oprah chewed him out in person on her show. She addressed her audience: "I made a mistake and I left the impression that the truth does not matter. And I am deeply sorry about that, because that is not is what I believe."

The Frey incident brought attention to a lack of fact-checking in the book publishing industry. Change was imminent. Said HarperCollins editor David Hirshey: "I think whether it is going to be a fig leaf or an honest attempt to make sure we are a bastion of accuracy, something is going to happen."[3]

Frey isn't the only fact faker to be exposed in recent years. Journalists have quoted bad sources, fabricated stories, and invented quotes. Incidences of lying nonfiction writers and journalists might make media cynics conclude that what we read in books, newspapers, and magazines cannot be trusted. The media critic, however, looks at the example of a writer caught in his lies and publicly savaged and sees a culture that cares about truthful information. That's a hopeful sign.

Print's Not Dead

A thousand years ago, manuscripts were written by hand. Because most humans could not read or write, poetry and philosophy texts were written out laboriously by trained scribes. These professionals spent their lives reproducing texts. Because so much labor was involved, a manuscript was a rare treasure. Access to manuscripts was confined to the elite.

Movable type (individual characters, letters, punctuation) emerged around 1000 CE in China. In Germany, Johannes Gutenberg invented a printing press that used movable type in the late 1400s. These technological innovations shifted culture. More printed texts and more readily available texts exposed more people to new ideas, experiences, and ways of thinking. Philosophy, history, scientific thought, and religious doctrines could be pondered by increasing numbers of those who could read and by increasing the population of the literate. Ultimately, gains in literacy would lead to revolutions from the Renaissance to the Enlightenment to the Internet Age.

In the United States today, an estimated 99 percent of the population over age 15 can read and write.[4] Despite rumors of print media's death, more than three-quarters of American adults say they read at least one book a year, according to Pew Research's "Snapshot of Reading in America in 2013." Pew reported that nearly 7 in 10 adults read a book in print in 2013 and more than one-quarter read an e-book.[5]

Even young adults are reading more magazines and books. A National Endowment for the Arts survey, "Reading on the Rise," reported a 21 percent increase in the reading rates of those ages 18 to 24.[6] Lots of books. Plenty of readers. We're reading books on mobile devices and tablets, true, but printed words on paper still attract wide audiences.

To some, words printed in newspapers, magazines, or books may seem trustworthy—unlike the fleeting electronic text posted on social networking sites. However, reports of fabrications—representing fictions as facts—demonstrate that the print medium boasts no intrinsic magic that makes its content more truthful than, say, a blog post. A book or magazine may promote ideas, industries, and individuals in ways that are less than completely independent. Some print media might influence less useful trends in culture. Because of this, print media's honesty, independence, and productivity need to be checked—as much as any other medium. When it comes to content, a critic applies the same HIP-factor tests to printed material as she does to YouTube videos, Wikipedia entries, or online news sources.

Since the range of print media includes everything from fiction books like *The Hunger Games* series to nonfiction fashion advice in *Cosmopolitan* to articles in your town's daily newspaper, the critic's work seems vast and sprawling. For this project, we'll look carefully at just a few of the successes, failures, and challenges of print journalism—the tradition of nonfiction reporting by paid professionals in books, magazines, and newspapers.

Honesty in Print

Remember the good old days when every news item or biography in newspapers or books was certifiably true? No, you don't. That's because the history of print media is checkered with episodes during which its attention (and commitment) to fact could be characterized as tenuous. In the 1890s, prominent newspapers in New York City owned by Joseph Pulitzer and William Randolph Hearst were battling for readers by printing exaggerated and often fabricated stories. This era of newspapering was dubbed "yellow journalism," named for a popular cartoon "The Yellow Kid" (which had characters drawn in yellow). The term *yellow journalism* came to be synonymous with sensational, often inaccurate, and manipulative journalism.

The term didn't apply to all newspapers. In 1896, the *New York Times* offered a stark contrast to yellow journalism.[7] The *Times* stuck to the facts, offering a sedate version of the nation's news. Its editors and reporters attempted to report and publish the most accurate version of events. A model was established for ethical journalism—sticking to the verifiable facts. These days, reporters who become inventive in their treatment of truth have lost their jobs and credibility.

- In 1981, *Washington Post* reporter Janet Cooke received a Pulitzer Prize for her story "Jimmy's World," a profile of an 8-year-old heroin addict. The problem? Jimmy didn't exist. When her fakery was discovered, the newspaper returned the prize. Cooke resigned from the paper.

- In 1998, journalist Stephen Glass was found to be inventing tall tales that were published as truthful reports in *The New Republic*.[8]

- In 2003, *New York Times* reporter Jayson Blair was fired for his faked and plagiarized "facts."

These examples of fakery seem to point to a dismal failure in book publishing, magazine, and newspaper industries in America. But they can also be seen as proof that these industries care enough about verifiable truth to expose liars.

In fact, thousands of book authors, magazine writers, and newspaper journalists work hard every day to give the public useful, accurate information. Most journalists adhere to a code of ethics that obligates them to report the truth in ways the public can understand. Veteran journalists Bill Kovach and Tom Rosenstiel describe truth telling as a core principle of journalism. Journalists gather and verify facts and report them accurately, without embellishment, changing nothing. "Do not add things that did not happen,"[9] the authors instruct. It's straightforward advice.

The "do not add" rule, at face value, seems an objective approach to reporting—a technique not influenced by personal opinion or bias. An honest journalist does his best to craft this honest report. That said, the journalist and the audiences *must* understand that none of the reporting, writing, and editing occurs without some influencing factors along the line. We use the word *objective* to describe a bias-free journalistic account. But the term *objectivity* is a tricky one for journalists working in any medium. It's tricky because news media depend on reporters and editors making many subjective decisions, choices that require value judgments, in the news-gathering, reporting, and publishing phases. A look at the reporting, writing, editing, and publication process helps show how difficult it might be to achieve "objectivity" in news—even honest news.

The process of selection begins when journalists choose what to cover out the thousands of potential stories. After being assigned or choosing a story, reporters make choices about where to obtain information and who to interview. When putting a story together, the reporter decides what facts and details to include or to leave out and what quotes to report or to paraphrase. Editors and designers determine how long the story will be and where it will appear in the paper—on the front page of a newspaper or website or buried deeper in the publication. So many choices need to be made, each choice guided by an individual's desire to tell a story that delivers information. These choices can make the news-gathering and disseminating process more subjective.

Many problems might emerge in this subjective news-gathering process. As noted in the last paragraph, reporters decide who they'll talk to, what sources they'll use for their reports. A problem emerges when the reporter talks to sources who provide unreliable information or misleading half-truths, whether because of ignorance or deliberately. This can happen at a student newspaper or at the newspaper noted above for being a fine example of ethical journalism—the *New York Times*.

In 2005, *New York Times* reporter Judith Miller left her job after allegations surfaced that she'd mishandled reporting on weapons of mass destruction, relying on unverified and inaccurate information passed along to her by a biased source. Her reporting contributed to the U.S. decision to invade Iraq in 2003.[10] Miller's stories turned out to be full of errors. No weapons of mass destruction were ever found in Iraq. Miller's biggest problem? The sources she chose for her stories were, at best, misinformed. At worst, sources used her to place disinformation in a well-respected newspaper in an attempt to generate public support for war.[11]

The blame for Miller's shoddy reporting wasn't hers alone. Editors approved the erroneous information that ended up on the front page of the *Times*. Miller finally resigned. The paper apologized for the faulty stories without laying total blame on Miller: "Editors at several levels who should have been challenging reporters and pressing for more skepticism were perhaps too intent on rushing scoops into the paper."[12]

The story seems to be another dismal example of dishonesty but take heart. Miller's reporting problems stand out because this is *not* the norm for print journalism. At their best, reporters and editors substantiate the information they plan to make public. An adage once taught in journalism schools suggested to new reporters: "If your mother says she loves you, check it out." When print journalists are done reporting and writing, editors and fact-checking departments come along to reverify facts and make sure opposing opinions are fairly represented.

Although accurate reporting is the goal, errors can easily end up being published at the best of online or print edition newspapers. When mistakes large and small are made, news media run corrections in print editions and change online content, adding notations, to reflect the most accurate information. Like many newspapers, the *New York Times* runs a list of corrections daily, noting everything from misspelled names to errors of fact.

One small example ran after the paper ran a story about the 2012 shooting of Trayvon Martin, an unarmed African American teenager, by a neighborhood watch volunteer George Zimmerman. The *Times* article reported incorrectly that Zimmerman made 46 emergency calls to 911 over 14 months. This error was repeated in two stories. In fact, Zimmerman made the calls over a period of eight years, the *Times* editors wrote in a later correction to both articles. The correction ran in the print edition and online. Both online stories were changed, and the changes were noted at the stories' ends.[13] This practice of publishing a list of mistakes and corrections adds to print journalism's credibility.

As a result of print journalism's commitment to accuracy and verification—and correcting errors when necessary— much of the public still tends to trust many mainstream media news outlets as sources of valid information. The acts of a few dishonest nonfiction writers and careless journalists are not the norm for print journalism. Indeed, that's why they stand out. Instead of provoking our cynicism, these examples help us see the value placed on truth in our society.

Independence of Print

Former *Washington Post* editor Ben Bradlee became famous for his feisty independence from any potential conflicts of interest. Bradlee didn't think journalists should belong to any special interest groups, not even a political party. That way, readers could never suspect the news of being biased. Ethical journalists, Bradlee said, also should not give money to causes or participate in any sort of activism— even on the weekend when they weren't being journalists. "Stay the hell out," he said of his advice to journalists. "Just don't belong to anything—best rule. Don't belong to anything. I don't belong to country clubs. I don't belong to anything."[14]

Bradlee was famously the editor who, in 1972, assigned Bob Woodward and Carl Bernstein to report on the story of a burglary of the headquarters of the Democratic National Committee at the Watergate office building in Washington, D.C. Their reporting led to the resignation of Republican president Richard Nixon, who'd lied to the American public about his involvement in illegal activities. Because of Bradlee's fiercely nonpartisan journalistic ethics, it would have been harder for the public to charge the *Washington Post* with bias. The investigative journalism that led to exposing the Watergate scandal was a high point in the history of American journalism.

Bradlee's approach seems sensible in light of the public's suspicions that news media are offering only part of a story—a story shaped to accommodate the biased leanings of, say, a political party or ideological perspective. Accusations of media bias fly from all directions. Bernard Goldberg complains of a liberal news media slant in his book *Bias*. That type of charge is refuted in Eric Alterman's well-researched book, *What Liberal Media?* Alterman contends that the media's business model can only mean an underlying conservative bias.

Maintaining independence from the sources of stories is a key journalistic principle, write Kovach and Rosenstiel. This applies to straight news stories, as well as opinion columns and reviews. That doesn't mean journalists need to be "objective," which we've seen is an elusive value. It does mean that the truth is sought out in a way that best serves the public interest. "It is this independence of spirit and mind, rather than neutrality, that the journalists must keep in focus."[15]

Bias comes in many forms that transcend liberal or conservative politics. Chapter One introduced media critics Edward Herman and Noam Chomsky, who write that media are filtered by the interests of media ownership, advertisers, sources, public feedback, and ideological correctness. These filters, write Herman and Chomsky, determine the kinds of stories covered by most news media. Print journalists are not exempt from concerns about losing advertisers by running stories unfavorable to an industry—or about losing readers by running stories that challenge or offend the audience. Newspapers, online and print, are most often for-profit businesses. And now, new media models—from YouTube to Twitter to websites where volunteer bloggers write for free—threaten the business of journalism. Sites like Craigslist fill the need once met by highly profitable classified ad sections in newspapers. Media companies face inevitable declines in readership, advertising rates, and, ultimately, profits.

Some good examples of independent print journalism come from outside the corporate media system. Authors Kovach and Rosenstiel note that the U.S. alternative press—smaller newsweeklies across the nation—are "a vibrant part of the journalism landscape" and even "closer to the historical roots of journalism than the large corporate-owned papers that often profess that they provide a neutral news account."[16] Just one example—the award-winning *Colorado Springs Independent*, privately owned by John Weiss, has won national awards for its investigative reporting and coverage of important issues, including immigration, health care, and education. The Association of Alternative Newsmedia (AAN), a group of more than 100 alternative news organizations, describes it like this: "No sacred cows. Balanced investigative reporting. Bold graphics. Crisp writing. Crusading columnists, often at odds with one another."[17] Across the nation, small newsweeklies cover the local government, people, and the arts scenes in their communities. AAN describes its members as having in common "a strong focus on local news, culture, and the arts; an informal and sometimes profane style; an emphasis on point-of-view reporting and narrative journalism; a tolerance for individual freedoms and social differences; and an eagerness to report on issues and communities that many mainstream media outlets ignore."[18]

Another example of a potentially independent publication might be found at your school. Scholastic journalism—high school and college news media in print and online—often includes engaging independent content not influenced by corporate ownership and less dependent on advertising. High school and college journalists, however, aren't immune from attempts at censorship—from school administrators, teachers, or even concerned parents—even over seemingly minor issues. But the Supreme Court has noted that the First Amendment protects students, arguing: "It can hardly be argued that either students or teachers shed their constitutional right to freedom of speech at the schoolhouse gate."[19] That quote comes from the 1969 Supreme Court decision supporting students who were protesting the Vietnam War by wearing black armbands at their Iowa public school. The students had been suspended for their symbolic act.

Complicating matters, though, is another U.S. Supreme Court decision, *Hazelwood School District v. Kuhlmeier* (1988) that gave public high school administrators some ability to censor student publications. The ruling requires school officials to show reasonable educational justification before censorship can occur, and the Court's decision doesn't apply to publications that have been opened as "public forums for student expression," advises the Student Law Press Center.[20]

The struggle for freedom of the press continues. When, in 2011, an editorial in an Illinois high school newspaper criticized the school's administration for being lax in enforcing dress codes and rules pertaining to cell phone use, all copies of the newspaper were confiscated. School administrators called the editors in for a meeting and told them to reprint the newspaper without the condemning editorial. The school's policy maintains: "School authorities may edit or delete material that is inconsistent with the District's educational mission." After that incident, school officials demanded to see the newspaper content before the paper went to print.[21]

Many interests compromise the absolute independence of print journalists. High school administrators don't want their school to look bad. A reporter covering city government needs to stay on good terms with the mayor just so she can do her job. Since print media are businesses, newspapers need to make money. Can't irritate advertisers. Despite these pressures, knowledgeable reporters and editors do their best to report and write without bias. These journalists know that they need to maintain independence to serve the public's interest and to fulfill journalism's watchdog role—to be the Fourth Estate, keeping track of the other three branches of U.S. government.

Productivity of Print

Journalists view themselves as serving both as watchdogs and as decoders, making complex issues, events, and institutions understandable to a wide audience. Together, by acting as informants and as interpreters, they play an indispensable role in helping citizens in a democracy.

The problem? For the past decade, the print journalism traditions in the United States have been in danger of extinction as journalism's business model shifts. One of the ways that newspapers made money in the past was by printing paid classified advertising. Before the 1990s, the only place people could list a car for sale or an apartment for rent was in the newspaper. Print publications made plenty of money, as well, from display advertising for national and local businesses. Although grocery store supplements are still crammed into local newspapers as of this writing, the rise of online advertising and websites like Craigslist, Backpage, Monster, CareerBuilder, and RealEstateFinder have made the newspaper industry much less profitable than it used to be. As a result, to keep making money, most newspaper chains have made extensive cuts to newsroom staffs. That's been taking a toll on the quantity and quality of investigative and interpretive journalism. Even author Clay Shirky, a cheerleading fan of new technology's potential as a useful information medium, worries about the decline of good reporting if what he calls the "old model" of newspapers goes away too soon. "I think we are headed into a long trough of decline in accountability journalism," Shirky writes, "because the old models are breaking faster than the new models can be put into place."[22]

Let's dig into print media productivity first by looking at some of print journalism's successes. Fairness and Accuracy in Reporting (FAIR), an advocacy group, was founded in 1986 "on the belief that journalism matters—that getting out the truth can improve the world, while news that distorts or denies reality can have terrible consequences."[23] The group lists numerous instances of investigating and reporting crimes and injustices of global importance—as well as some instances of bad reporting that have also had dramatic consequences. Here are some useful examples:

- In 1986, when Ronald Reagan was president, Associated Press reporters uncovered facts revealing that the United States had been secretly and illegally funding a rebel army, the Nicaraguan Contras, to take down the Sandinista government in Nicaragua. Stories by the *Washington Post* then emerged that linked the U.S. operation to funds from illegal sales of weapons to Iran. Yes, the United States once sold weapons to the same Iran that seems threatening today. Nine people were convicted in the Iran-Contra affair as it came to be known.

- In 1996, Northwestern University journalism students were responsible for the release of the Ford Heights Four, four African American men who were found to have been wrongfully convicted of a double murder. The investigative efforts of students and their professor uncovered DNA evidence that did not match up—and led to the arrest of the real killers. Two of the wrongfully convicted men had faced the death penalty. Each of the four innocent men had spent 18 years in jail.[24]

- In 1998, an Associated Press article about Matthew Shepard, beaten to death in Laramie, Wyoming, paved the way for mainstream press coverage of violence toward and discrimination against the gay community.

- In 2003, the torture of detainees by the U.S. military at Iraqi prison Abu Ghraib was reported in an investigative *New Yorker* article by Seymour Hersh and on CBS's *60 Minutes*.

These stories are just a few of the many, many stories reported each day, all of which exemplify the importance of news media in shining a light down those dark alleys where misdeeds occur. But these influential investigative stories are relatively rare. The bulk of the stories covered by news media daily help us understand our elected representatives and public officials. Every day, journalists drive around your town, make phone calls, and send emails. They report on events and issues that range from the mundane to the exceptional. Journalists cover key topics—explaining how public money is spent, how law enforcement officials handle crime, and how education leaders decide what to teach in schools. Knowing more about topics that affect their lives helps people understand what's going on in their worlds.

Reporters play key roles in a society that depends on informed citizens having access to verifiable facts presented in a digestible form. That's why so many of us cringe when hearing that about 37,000 newspaper jobs have been lost since 2008.[25]

Can verifiable, accountable journalism of the kind done by trained journalists survive without print newspapers to support the reporting? That's the question of our online era. Certainly, the productive art of journalism deserves the support of online news media venues and aggregators. Google CEO Eric Schmidt notes: "Well-funded, targeted professionally managed investigative journalism is a necessary precondition, in my view, to a functioning democracy."[26] Google is often cited as one of the factors in journalism's demise. Less reported are Google's efforts to work with newspapers to optimize the business model. Schmidt emphasizes that Google's survival depends on partnerships with information gatherers like newspapers, magazines, and broadcast journalists.

The medium for investigative journalism is shifting. The Schmidt interview wasn't a newspaper report. The story ran on a blog, Search Engine Land. The estimate of newspaper jobs lost is based on the counting work of Erica

Smith, a social media editor at the *St. Louis Post-Dispatch*, who presented her research on her blog. The Smoking Gun website did the reporting that led to Oprah's public denunciation of Frey's fake memoir. Many positive indicators point to a robust future for reporters and information gatherers who perform a watchdog role—even if the medium shifts from print on paper to pixels on a screen.

Productivity? Whether reporting and writing in print or online, journalists rock our world.

BE THE CRITIC

- Look up the past week's worth of corrections in the *New York Times* online edition, http://www.nytimes.com/pages/corrections/index.html. Create a spreadsheet to record what types of mistakes the paper makes and the language it uses to correct them.

- Read transcripts of Jim Lehrer's interview with Ben Bradlee on *PBS Newshour* at http://www.pbs.org/newshour/bradlee/background_ethics.html. Take the online journalism ethics quiz based on Bradlee's ethical position. Do you agree with Bradlee's insistence that an ethical journalist should never join anything or participate in public life?

- Find examples of productive print journalism in your local or school newspaper or online news media. How has reporting changed the environment in which you live—or how has it failed to do so?

SATIATE YOUR CURIOSITY

- Check out resources for scholastic journalism at the Student Law Press Center, get to know your First Amendment rights, and poke around through recent news and updates. http://www.splc.org

- Watch *Shattered Glass*, a movie that dramatizes the story of *The New Republic* reporter Stephen Glass, who was fired for fabricating several stories. Be sure to watch the *60 Minutes* interview with the real Stephen Glass, a bonus feature on the movie's DVD.

- Check out The Smoking Gun's story "A Million Little Lies: Exposing James Frey's Fiction Addiction." The website investigated claims made in James Frey's memoir, a book that Oprah Winfrey had promoted on her show. http://www.thesmokinggun.com/documents/celebrity/million-little-lies

- The *PBS Frontline* four-part series "News Wars" examines news media trends and problems in the United States. Newspapers still play a key role in journalism, the documentary contends, because print journalists working at newspapers do more original reporting than those working in any other medium. The first part begins by examining the conflicted story of Judith Miller at the *New York Times* and ends with the story of how ownership changes affected the *Los Angeles Times*. http://www.pbs.org/wgbh/pages/frontline/newswar/

Parody News

"I've existed in this country forever. There have been people like me who satirize the political process and who have satirized—what was it that Will Rogers said? 'How crazy is it when politicians are a joke and comedians are taken seriously?'"

> —*The Daily Show*'s Jon Stewart, speaking to Chris Wallace of Fox News

In May 2011, U.S. military and intelligence forces killed Osama bin Laden, the al Qaeda leader considered responsible for terrorist acts including the September 11, 2001, attack on the World Trade Center in New York City. U.S. international news media covered the story. So did the parody news show, *The Daily Show with Jon Stewart*.[1]

The Daily Show's "Afghan Bureau Chief" Aasif Manvi reported from what appeared to be Afghanistan. He complained about the remote mountainous place where Osama bin Laden had been thought to be hiding. "Turns out the son-of-a-bitch was living in the suburbs!" Manvi exclaimed. "Osama bin 'Trust Fund' was living two miles from a golf course. I could have embedded myself in the fourteenth fairway!"

Of course, Manvi was not a bureau chief for a news organization and he was not in Afghanistan. The comedian's remarks were filmed in front of a green screen in a New York TV studio. Creators of *The Daily Show with Jon Stewart* consider themselves to be entertainers, not journalists. The show takes real news events and creates parody news segments about issues, events, politicians, and celebrities.

A cynic might dismiss comedy news shows as mere fakery, but parody and satire have played a key role in political discourse and social reform for more than 2,000 years. A media critic looks carefully at contemporary parody news to gauge its usefulness in a balanced media diet.

Parody and Satire

At their best, parody news programs use satire, a type of humor that relies on sarcasm, ridicule, and irony (saying one thing but meaning the exact opposite) to expose absurdities and to reveal hypocrisy, stupidity, and ignorance. For example, *The Daily Show* mocked cable news pundits by having young children read transcripts from shows on Fox News and MSNBC.[2] That's parody, a humorous imitation. Removed from the context of serious cable news show and delivered by young children, the comments made by adults sound truly juvenile. That's satire, imitation that reveals the silliness of, in this case, what passes for political debate in contemporary media.

The use of satire dates back, at least, to Plato's transmission of the dialogues of Greek philosopher Socrates and the witty, politically scathing works of Roman poets Horace and Juvenal. Writers from several cultures have parodied epic literature and satirized information and ideas propounded by monarchs, religious leaders, revolutionaries, and even scientists. In the United States, the *New York Sun*, the first newspaper created for the masses, expanded its readership in the 1830s by offering sensational and occasionally fake news content. In one series, a reporter described "scientific" discoveries of bat-winged humanoids on the moon. Decades later, at a newspaper on the Western frontier, humorist Mark Twain parodied the *Sun* and other popular papers by writing "news stories" about a petrified man found in a silver mine and a fictitious bloody massacre near Carson City, Nevada.

In the 1930s, film giant Metro-Goldwyn-Mayer produced comedic newsreels that combined real news footage with humorous commentary. In 1975, NBC launched *Saturday Night Live*, a show that mocked U.S. culture and politics through skits and fake news broadcasts. In 1988, two University of Wisconsin students created *The Onion*, a parody newspaper that grew to include award-winning online and broadcast news parodies. *The Daily Show* premiered in 1996; Jon Stewart stepped in as the show's faux anchor in 1999. Stephen Colbert was a *Daily Show* regular until he started a show of his own, *The Colbert Report*, in 2005.

These days, more young people watch parody news than watch CNN or read the *New York Times*. While only about one-third of TV news viewers ages 18–49 tune into nightly news broadcasts, about 80 percent watch Stewart, according to a 2010 Pew poll.[3] The top three "news" sources for this demographic include *The Colbert Report* (80%), *The Daily Show* (74%), and the *New York Times* (67%).

Many viewers in the under-50 demographic consider Stewart to be a trusted news source. In a 2007 Pew Research Center for the People & the Press poll that asked people to name the "journalist" they "most admired," comedian

Stewart was named about as often as broadcast news veterans Brian Williams (NBC), Tom Brokaw (NBC), and Anderson Cooper (CNN).[4]

What do viewers like about fake news? For starters, it keeps you rolling on the floor laughing. Although parody news shows make no claim to be news media, at their best, these shows can help keep citizens informed. After carefully observing the content of parody news programs, a critic assesses their usefulness by asking three questions. Is the medium honest? Is it independent? Is it productive?

Is Parody News Honest?

News reporters pay careful attention to facts—recording and reporting accurately and in context. At their best, operating independently and subject to verification, news reporters strive to be truthful. Parody news, however, is not truthful in the literal sense. Comedians are pretending to be journalists, pretending to go places but never leaving the studio. Can a medium be honest without sticking to the literal truth?

In her essay, "The Fake News as the Fifth Estate," Rachel Sotos compares Stewart with Greek philosopher Socrates, who feigned ignorance and engaged in dialogues with contemporary leaders. "Through [Stewart's] ironic reports, he presses the logic of his interlocutors to their illogical extremes," Sotos writes. "Like Socrates, Stewart often reveals the gap between a reasonable view of things and the quite dangerous assumptions of those in power and pompously claiming to be experts."[5] Although *The Daily*

Show's content isn't strictly truthful, Sotos argues that it is honest, perhaps even more honest than other media.

Instead of offering stories about celebrity baby daddies as news or serving up a dire nightly mix of crime, silly pet stories, and natural disaster coverage, fake news may help audiences see the shallow nature of some news traditions. Parody news shows operate as a new kind of public guardian, Sotos suggests, a watchdog that observes and comments on media institutions. The media serve as the "fourth estate," a watchdog over the three "estates" or three branches of government (executive, legislative, and judicial). Parody news, disguised as nonthreatening humorous content, glides under the radar, offering commentary not only on three branches of government but on other media as well. That's why Sotos calls parody news the "fifth estate." It may not be literally truthful, but its satire provides honest insights into the nature of today's news media.

The Daily Show has won 16 Emmy awards for its entertainment value—it has also received two Peabody awards, prestigious journalism prizes, for campaign coverage in 2000 and 2004. The show also won the Orwell Award for Distinguished Contribution to Honesty and Clarity in Public Language in 2005. Judges praised *The Daily Show*, which they said had "armed increasing numbers of watchers (through the sharp edge of humor) with rhetorical tools for seeing their way through the fog."[6]

Viewers today need tools to see through the fog of entertainment, news, and information media. Shows like *The Daily Show* may look, at first, like mindless fun for young audiences. But its content clearly helps us better understand absurdities in our media, our political system, and our society.

Is Parody News Independent?

Independent news media are free from censorship by government, by corporate ownership, and by advertisers. They are free from ideological pressures or bias, operating to provide the most honest, accurate, and verifiable information—even if this information challenges or contradicts previously held beliefs. An independent media source would offer straightforward information that might help humans better understand our world. As might be guessed, an independent unbiased media source is hard to find.

Jon Stewart has charged Fox News with being a "relentless agenda-driven 24-hour news opinion propaganda delivery system."[7] Fox News anchor Chris Wallace interviewed Stewart in 2011, accusing Stewart of having a biased liberal agenda. Stewart admitted to Wallace that *The Daily Show* does not "tell the full story" but argued that the show's filtering mechanism has little to do with being liberal or conservative. "I don't *not* tell the full story based on a purely ideological partisan agenda," Stewart told Wallace. *The Daily Show*'s agenda, Stewart said, is to reveal absurdity in the political process and in the mass media. "That is the agenda that we push. It is anticorruption, anti-lack-of-authenticity, and anti-contrivance. I see that more in one area than another. Our main thrust is comedic."[8]

At first glance, a media critic might suspect that a parody news show running on a corporate-owned cable television channel may not be able to offer content that's independent of the company's interests. The example of *The Daily Show* demonstrates some complications with this assumption. The show runs on Comedy Central, a cable channel owned by Viacom, which is controlled by a larger company—National Amusements. The company's founder is billionaire Sumner Redstone, now executive chairman of the boards of Viacom and National Amusements.

So Redstone is the boss. What would seem unlikely is that Stewart might produce content that challenges or even reveals the business practices of Viacom, the company that owns his show, or of Sumner Redstone, the company's founder. Yet, in past *Daily Show* episodes, Stewart has covered stories involving Viacom and Redstone. When Viacom sued YouTube in 2007 for running its copyrighted content (including clips from *The Daily Show*), Stewart called in the show's pop culture "expert" Demetri Martin to explain the lawsuit. Martin used stick puppets of Redstone and the Google founders to illustrate the lawsuit. He suggested that the winner might be the company with more money, noting that Viacom was worth $25 billion at the time—while spuriously proposing Google's worth at "something like $14 trillion." Martin said, wryly, that Google's founders were planning a gold-plated rock-climbing wall in their office.[9]

In the comedic bit, Viacom comes out looking good. So Stewart may not exactly be biting the hand that feeds him in these stories. Because his paychecks come from Viacom, Stewart perhaps observes a line that he and his staff of writers should not cross. But the fact that he's a comedian might allow him to play with the line a bit more than, say, an investigative news reporter for CBS—also owned by National Amusements. A comedy routine that involves Redstone as a stick figure is funny. Even billionaires wouldn't want to be perceived as not being able to take a joke. Is Stewart's show independent of censorship and bias? Stewart admits to an agenda that seeks to reveal absurdity. He talks less about the fact that he works for a gigantic media corporation that pays him millions.[10] In considering the independence of a popular parody news broadcast, the media critic also needs to look carefully at the impact of media ownership—even on comedy shows.

Is Parody News Productive?

The last question to ask of parody news involves its ability to inform its audience and to have a positive impact on society. Does it produce increased awareness and social change?

Regular viewers of parody news programs turn out to be more informed than many other news audiences, according to national studies. In 2004, the Annenberg Public Policy Center of the University of Pennsylvania reported that viewers of late-night parody news shows knew more about election issues and candidates' positions during that election cycle than those who didn't watch the late-night comedies.[11] In 2007, Pew researchers surveyed the political knowledge of 1,502 people on issues from minimum wage hikes to the fact that more civilians than troops had died in Iraq.[12] The Pew team reported that *The Daily Show* and *Colbert Report* viewers had more knowledge about public affairs than any other news audience—they even had a slight edge over those who listen to National Public Radio. Parody news informs viewers, giving us news in a digestible form.

Both Colbert and Stewart invite influential figures like politicians, economists, actors, authors, and national leaders—from Bruce Springsteen to Bill Clinton—to appear on their shows. When Barack Obama appeared on Stewart's show on October 29, 2008, around 3.6 million viewers tuned in.[13] Before the 2010 midterm elections, Colbert and Stewart held opposing "rallies" in Washington, D.C., attracting tens of thousands of people to both "Rally to Restore Sanity" (Stewart) and "Rally to Keep Fear Alive" (Colbert). These rallies were not about promoting a particular candidate or partisan agenda. Rather, the comedians called on their audiences to stand up and help shape public discourse in new and more useful ways.[14]

Colbert gained media attention for proposing a political action committee or SuperPAC to fund campaign activities for the 2012 elections. His SuperPAC was approved by the Federal Election Commission, which allowed the comedian the same rights given to corporations as a result of the Supreme Court's 2010 *Citizens United* decision. He could raise and spend unlimited money on the 2012 elections. By using his SuperPAC to air ridiculous commercials, Colbert called attention to the social irresponsibility of unfettered corporate spending on elections. By pretending to consider running for president and passing the SuperPAC's control to Stewart, Colbert made us realize the danger and unfair impact of SuperPACs.

Colbert uses his comedy as a platform for reform. In 2010, Colbert testified in character before Congress about the day he spent picking beans and corn with immigrant farmworkers.[15] When Rep. Judy Chu (D–CA) asked Colbert why he chose to get involved in this issue, he shed his egotistical character. "I feel the need to speak for those who can't speak for themselves," Colbert told the committee and the media. Colbert, a Roman Catholic, quoted words attributed to Jesus in the New Testament, "Whatever you did for one of the least of these brothers of mine, you did for me." In these dark economic times, Colbert noted, many people could be considered among "the least," but migrant farmworkers work hard, suffer mistreatment, and have no rights. As he pointed this out, Colbert is doing what journalists have sought to do—keeping an ear to the ground for the cries of the oppressed. He's also making full use of his position as a member of the Fifth Estate.

In discussing the Fifth Estate, Sotos suggests that fake news provides more opportunities for people to become truly knowledgeable and to engage as political activists. "The fake news is not only—in its own way—more true to the facts, it's closer to the cutting edge of new possibilities for political participation," Sotos writes.[16] That's productive.

BE THE CRITIC

Does comedy news help citizens become better-informed participants in our democracy? You be the judge.

- Pick three shows in a similar time period. For each show, record the first five stories you hear. Don't be selective—just grab the first five.

- Write down some of the details in the stories you watch. Is the news parody honest, if not entirely truthful? If facts are used, are the facts verifiable? Are the media makers deliberately trying to mislead the public or is a larger issue at stake?

- Does the parody content seem independent of bias? Bias might come from censorship by media owners, advertisers, or audiences. Can you tell if the "full story" is being told? What might be left out? Why?

- Finally, was this material productive? Did any change result from new knowledge or awareness? Does the story affect you personally in any way? Do you feel inspired to think, act, or understand in different ways?

- Based on its honesty, independence, and productive nature, give the shows your seal of approval—or not.

- You did the work of being a media critic. Now, share your results. Communicate your research to friends, family members, and classmates. Make a poster for the halls of your school. Send an email to the producers of parody news. Don't let your hard-won knowledge go to waste.

SATIATE YOUR CURIOSITY

- In 2006, Jon Stewart appeared on an episode of CNN's debate show, *Crossfire*, and skewered the show's hosts. His criticism was so pertinent that it was named by show producers as one reason that *Crossfire* was discontinued. The clip lives in numerous places online, including YouTube. http://www.youtube.com/watch?v=aFQFB5YpDZE

- Stephen Colbert spoke about truthiness just a
  few feet from Pres. George W. Bush at a Washington Press Correspondents' annual dinner, also in
  2006. The entire hilarious talk is archived at Google
  videos. http://video.google.com/videoplay?do
  cid=-869183917758574879

- Pew Research Center for People & the Press surveys
  people about their media habits and has found that
  young people often get news from late-night comedy
  shows. More survey: http://www.people-press.org

Social Networks

"It is no longer possible to adopt the aloof and dissociated role of the literate Westerner."

—Marshall McLuhan, *Understanding Media: The Extensions of Man*

"I'm going to the occupy wall street protests in philly this week. I'm stoked to be a part of something as opposed to just facebooking it"

—posted to Twitter by WeHateTucker, October 1, 2011

In the 1980s, well before social online networks emerged, two award-winning filmmakers created a script for a 30-second eco-activist TV commercial. The animated ad showed a sapling engaged in heartfelt conversation with Grandpa—a giant of the forest. The ad's goal was to save old-growth forests.

Filmmakers Bill Schmalz and Kalle Lasn, who later founded the *Adbusters* media activist publication, however, ran into a problem when TV stations rejected the commercial. The TV stations said they wouldn't run advocacy advertisements.[1] So, to save trees, activists had to rely on direct-action campaigns—hoping to attract the attention of the mainstream media. A few rugged individuals would camp out for weeks or even, in the case of activists like writer Julia Butterfly Hill, years in the branches of ancient redwoods, hoping to save trees from the saw blade and ax—and get a mention in TV news programs.

Times changed. Now anyone with an Internet connection and an urge to share thoughts, ideas, or recipes can upload a video to YouTube, link to it from Facebook, and promote it on Twitter. A citizen media maker has the power to craft a video that could be viewed 100 million times. A nonprofit political group possesses the same power. So does a large corporation. And so does a country's government. Social networks boast plenty of potential energy—in ways that seem, at first, to be fair and democratic.

Today, Lasn and Schmalz's 1980s "Talking Rainforest" commercial is available online. The Adbusters group's early experience with media censorship fueled two decades of media activism, from Lasn's popular book manifesto *Culture Jam* (2000) to the ad-free *Adbusters* magazine and website. Nowadays, *Adbusters* is perhaps best known for its role in sparking a nationwide Occupy Wall Street social protest in fall 2011.

Are social networks useful as agents of change? That's a key question facing media critics who invest the time to look closely at media messages, influences, and control. Overall, the social media landscape is altering so quickly that measuring its impact has proved difficult. The extent to which social networks offer honest, independent, and productive content might vary wildly and must be evaluated on a case-by-case basis.

It's arguable that, as in the case of *Adbusters* founders, social media are giving voice to those who would otherwise lack access to a mass audience. Interviewed on a late-night comedy show, Change.org founder Ben Rattrey talked about how some activist causes go "viral"—spreading online petitions like wildfire. "The power people have now to make a difference with social media is more than ever before," Rattrey said.[2]

At the same time, others argue that social media create more "slacktivists" than activists—people who simply push the "like" button and feel engaged. "The evangelists of social media . . . seem to believe that a Facebook friend is the same as a real friend," wrote Malcolm Gladwell in *The New Yorker.* "Facebook activism succeeds not by motivating people to make a real sacrifice but by motivating them to do the things that people do when they are not motivated enough to make a real sacrifice."[3] Gladwell contrasted online activism with civil rights protests of the 1960s, which involved activists risking arrest and beatings (and sometimes their lives) to make their point about equal access on buses and at lunch counters.

Gladwell's essay was published in 2010. Since then, participation in beyond-the-screen events has fueled hope that social movements can and do rise from interlinked online networks of friends and acquaintances. Occupy Wall Street protests were not confined to New York City but spread across the nation to the West Coast, Alaska, and Hawaii in 2011. Social media were cited as an important tool leading to political change in Egypt and other countries in the Middle East that year.

The power of social networks has become a concern for some governments, which have blocked access or attempted to censor social media. During the 2014 elections in Turkey, the government so feared the influence of social media that it attempted to block users' access to Twitter and YouTube. Turkey's Twitter ban was lifted after a Turkish court ruled that the ban violated that country's free speech guarantees.

The potential for a democratic shake-up of the people, for the people, by the people certainly seems to exist. But that possibility exists alongside the ability of governments and less-than-democratic political organizations to use the same social media tools for their own persuasive goals. In the 2014 wake of what's been characterized as "an occupation" of Ukraine by neighboring Russia, hundreds of thousands of people watched a video produced by the Russian government that depicted an alternate reality. "The unusually slick video, which has more than 500,000 YouTube views, appears to show exactly the opposite of what the world has witnessed in recent weeks," reported Cristina Corbin of Fox News. "Instead of Russia invading Crimea and even sending troops into other regions of eastern Ukraine, the video portrays Ukraine invading Russia's western provinces."[4] Corbin interviewed experts who deemed the video to be sophisticated propaganda.

Another complication of social media: the mainstream press has come to depend on YouTube, Twitter, Facebook, and other social media as reporting resources. Writes media critic Eric Louw: "what we have witnessed during the Arab Spring in general and the Syrian conflict in particular is that many mainstream media organizations have been all too willing to use the material posted to the Web by political activists, NGOs and citizen journalists often without verifying its contents."[5] Since no barriers exist to keep dishonest media from finding their way online, to use them without verification is irresponsible, to say the least.

When are social media at their best? Just like other media, social media can be examined for theirs honesty, independence, and productivity.

Here Come Social Media

In 1971, the first electronic mail was sent between two computers sitting next to each other. In 1978, online bulletin board systems (BBS) became the first electronic social networks on the Internet, a network of linked computers first funded by the military, then used by universities and research institutions. Users could post messages and share files on a BBS like Usenet, famous as the source for downloading the first Internet browser prototypes. Those first browsers, vehicles for getting around on what was being called the "information superhighway," were hard to use. Navigating vast amounts of information in cyberspace was tedious until 1990, when British physicist Tim Berners-Lee invented hypertext markup language or HTML. This programming language gave users a new interlinked way to present and find information online. The World Wide Web had been born.

By the early 1990s, web browsers included graphics and buttons that served as links to other information and pages. Websites were popping up everywhere. If you couldn't figure out how to use HTML, a company formed in 1994, Geocities, gave you easy tools to build a website of your own.

In 1995, a proto-Facebook site, The Globe, began offering users a chance to add customized content and link with others with similar interests. In 1997, a company. SixDegrees, added user profiles and "friends," a concept that Friendster put to good use in 2002. Friendster signed up three million users in three months, inspiring many imitators.

One clone was MySpace, set up in 2003, which quickly became the most-visited social network site at the time. In 2005, the site sold for $580 million to billionaire Rupert Murdoch of News Corporation, the media conglomerate that owns Fox News and other properties.[6] By 2008, the website's popularity had been eclipsed[7] by the new kid on the block—Facebook. In December 2011, Facebook reported that it had 845 million monthly active users,[8] making it the third-largest "nation" in the world.[9] Micro-blogging site Twitter, launched in 2006, offers its users unlimited posts of limited length, 140 characters. The company reported more than 100 million active users in 2011, who together sent an average of 230 million "tweets" per day.[10]

The huge popularity of Facebook and Twitter coincided with developments in smartphones that made it easy to post updates and tweet from anywhere—school, work, a protest in Cairo, or an occupation of Wall Street in New York. The communications world shifted on its axis. The whole world was watching.

The changes didn't happen overnight. But the result is that our access to a world of information is wider and more complicated than ever before. Social networks present a huge challenge to the media critic, who must find ways to sort through information online.

Are Social Media Honest?

Social networks are often the first place young people look for breaking news or entertainment. In 2010, the Pew Research Center reported that, for the first time, the Internet surpassed television as the main source of national and international news for people under 30.[11] When there's a natural disaster in another part of the country or the world, social networkers might hear about it online before it hits the news.

Like newspaper articles and TV news, a social network status update can be a timely, relevant "report." Thus, anyone who posts to Facebook is acting as a reporter. Even an Instagram photo of a friend's lunch is timely and local, and a person's healthful food choices could be said to have consequence. Perhaps a building next to a friend's workplace caught on fire. The friend posts photos and offers observations. Will her update be an accurate and useful report? How will such reports be verified? The latter—checking facts—is critical to journalistic traditions. But on social networks, millions of untrained new reporters may not know how to sort reliable sources from hearsay and speculation.

Misinformation spreads online easily. Much-reported social media hoaxes include false Amber alerts, erroneous information about California's gay marriage law, and celebrity deaths. Hoaxes can be passed along to hundreds or thousands of social networkers. ABC News quoted the TechCrunch blog: "While [Twitter] is great at disseminating information quickly, it's just as good at disseminating false information quickly. And if a lot of people are saying it—as thousands are here—it must be true, right? Wrong."[12]

The good news? A spate of Twitter hoaxes in 2009 led to awareness of the need for basic journalistic practices. The adage for reporters, "If your mother says she loves you, check it out," came back into play for Facebook posters and reTweeters. Before passing along an Amber alert, for example, the *Mashable Twitter Guidebook* advises checking with the National Center for Missing and Exploited Children online database.[13] That's exactly the kind of verification that journalists demand.

Careful users of social media know that misinformation hurts a social networker's reputation. A netiquette website advises that social media mistakes should be corrected quickly and in a transparent way to show what the person learned and how he learned it. This helps users maintain online credibility. Social networks, at their best, exemplify the power of the interconnected "hive" mind. Together, we are smarter.

As noted previously, newspapers run corrections in print or online editions as soon as possible after the mistake is identified and the factual information obtained. In print, the mistake is corrected a day or more later. As for books, if something's wrong with a book, well, how often do you hear of a book "recall" because of factual errors or missing information? James Frey's *A Million Little Pieces* could still be purchased at Amazon.com well after Oprah bawled him out publicly for his lies and fabrications.

A couple of obvious caveats: the makers and owners of social networks enjoy a high degree of centralized control, which we'll address in the next section on independence. The amount of freedom that social network users have is directly linked to what's being allowed by the owners of these computer tools. Also, public relations firms use social networks for advertising and promotional campaigns. Increasingly, young people are especially aware of these efforts and wary of any "friends" who seem to have ulterior motives.

Overall, however, the opportunity exists for social networks to not only offer raw, unfiltered honesty but to verify facts in real time as an event or life circumstance unfolds.

Are Social Media Independent?

To look at independence in social media, a critic might study its users, the companies behind the services, and the larger public entities at work to control and sometimes block online information. The Occupy Wall Street movement exemplified some of the strengths of social networking as an independent medium. In the summer of 2011, Adbusters announced activist plans in its print magazine and on its website. The plan was to Occupy Wall Street (OWS) in New York City in September and to take a stand on the influence of corporate wealth in U.S. politics. These plans were shared and multiplied exponentially through social networks. The #occupywallstreet project went viral, with messages tweeted and posted to Facebook. Across the nation, hundreds gathered at protest sites and thousands more watched supportively from the online sidelines.

The social media portions of OWS campaigns were not promoted by corporate media companies. No advertisers were enlisted as commercial sponsors for OWS's live streaming video. In fact, because of social networks, activists did not need to rely on mainstream news media as the sole means of conveying their messages. Activists broadcast the first videos of protesters being pepper-sprayed in California and live-streamed footage as police arrests activists on the Brooklyn Bridge in New York. So social networks can, to some extent, offer perspectives that reside outside the status quo and independent of censorship.

At the same time, independence can be limited, quite easily, with the flip of a computer server switch or by using filters that alter the flow of digital information. It can happen at the government level in countries like China, where the officials block websites and social network posts that discuss forbidden topics, including references to the Dalai Lama, the 1989 crackdown on Tiananmen Square protesters, and Falun Gong, the banned religious group. Since 2010, Internet users in China could not search for the word *freedom* online, reported the *New York Times*.[14] Media critic Seth Finkelstein, who's studied Internet censorship globally, concludes, "Contrary to earlier utopian theories of the Internet, it takes very little effort for governments to cause certain information simply to vanish for a huge number of people."[15]

Websites and content control also happen at the corporate level, when a search engine blocks sites from showing up in searches. Sometimes the ability to limit access to exploitive, hateful, or illegal information seems useful. Google and Microsoft have both developed software to block searches for objectionable content.[16] Content rules govern user posts to video sites like YouTube, photo-sharing sites, and social media networks. As media companies craft and enforce their own rules for content, outcomes seem arbitrary and not all that transparent to some. Critics aren't sure what content is being filtered, how often, or how the decisions are made.

Scores of workers labor around the clock to monitor social network content for companies like Facebook.[17] Workers delete a wide gamut of posts, from photos with violent or sexual content to hate speech, animal abuse, suicide threats, or any information promoting self-harm. Posts about eating disorders, self-mutilation, and "hard drug abuse" will be blocked, according to Facebook's "Community Standards."[18] This seems great—until a user realizes how easy it might be ban political speech, controversial opinions, and artworks.

That's arguably what happened when Facebook removed posts by the American Civil Liberties Union in 2013. An ACLU attorney says Facebook removed a photo from the ACLU's post about a controversial piece of art. The photo showed a statue in a public park outside Kansas City. The statue showed "a nude woman taking a selfie of her own exposed bronze breasts," attorney Lee Rowland writes. Shortly after the photo was posted, it disappeared from Facebook. The ACLU was blocked from posting for 24 hours and received a message from Facebook warning that this was the consequence for repeated violations of its policy. The social network had perhaps chosen the worst organization to pick on. The ACLU sues organizations and governments for free speech and other human rights violations. "Look, we're the ACLU," Rowland writes. "Of course our Facebook posts are going to touch on controversial subjects—if they didn't, we just wouldn't be doing our jobs."[19]

The media critic concludes, perhaps, that social networks offer individuals what seem like independent platforms for communication. Even ideas outside the norm might find a means of expression—but only up to a certain point. Threats to social media independence can come from governments or media companies. Media critics need to remain vigilant for such possible infringements on independence.

Are Social Media Productive?

OK, it's true. Facebook use can easily chew up hours of time that might otherwise be spent doing homework, practicing a musical instrument, hanging out with friends, or exercising. Many of us spend all too much time basking in the glow of a computer monitor, where we are stumbling upon various exciting bits of web content. This seems not at all productive. That said, the potential exists for social media to inform and even to prompt action from users. The use of social media during the revolutionary wave of protests known as the "Arab Spring" and by the Occupy Wall Street protesters exemplify attempts to use social media productively. Perhaps neither achieved the results for which organizers might have wished. But the potential of social media as a productive tool was becoming evident.

In Tunisia, when protests began in December 2010, videos of police brutality posted to Facebook outraged audiences and inspired activism. Videos were posted to Facebook because the government had blocked access to other video-sharing sites like YouTube. Attempts to ban and block Facebook in Tunisia were unsuccessful, thanks to "hacktivists" who used their Internet skills to subvert the Tunisian government's Internet control. Activism in Tunisia led to the dictatorial president fleeing within a month, the ousting of a corrupt political party within a few months, and the promise of democratic elections within a year. Those who felt Internet resources had made a difference in

Tunisia's struggle for democracy credited social networks for playing a role in the revolution.

The occupiers of U.S. cities, from Oakland, California, to Washington, D.C., say that they were inspired by social network–aided revolutions around the world, like those of the Arab Spring. Overall, did Occupy Wall Street accomplish its goals? It certainly created a national discussion about the economic plight of the 99 percent of the populace versus the 1 percent of individuals said to control most of the nation's wealth. It's hard to draw a direct correlation in some cases. But, in unrelated news a few months after the Occupiers had gone home, some activists pointed to increased awareness as a factor in a shareholder vote against a $15 million pay package for the chief executive officer of Citigroup. It was considered to be the first nixing of executive compensation in the banking institution's history. The shift, some argued, might even point to a change in the way the shareholders of corporate stock view income inequality and the "lavish salaries" of company heads.[20] Did increased awareness make a difference? We'd like to think so.

Adbusters founders couldn't get an ad on TV in the 1980s. But in the Occupied Fall of 2011, the group was broadcasting its messages far more widely and much less expensively, mostly through social media. Because the whole world was watching via the Internet and social media sites, TV networks that once might have balked at environmental activist ads in the 1980s ended up covering the event as news. That's the productive potential of social networks.

BE THE CRITIC

Immerse yourself in a debate over social media's revolutionary role. Start with award-winning journalist and author Malcolm Gladwell's essay "Small Change: Why The Revolution Will Not Be Tweeted" in *The New Yorker* (http://www.newyorker.com/reporting/2010/10/04/101004fa_fact_gladwell). Gladwell, in part, critiques the enthusiasm of social network cheerleader Clay Shirky, author of *Here Comes Everybody: The Power of Organizing Without Organizations*. Continue your exploration of the debate by reading Shirky's defense of social media optimism on his blog, http://www.shirky.com/weblog/, and on Twitter, @cshirky.

- Describe the basic arguments that Gladwell and Shirky make.

- Ask what values the two writers share.

- Look for credible, verifiable examples with which Gladwell and Shirky make their points.

- Evaluate the arguments based on the evidence you've found.

SATIATE YOUR CURIOSITY

- Watch a video that debates "Social Networks, Social Revolution." This episode of *Empire*, broadcast on *Al Jazeera English* in February 2011, sums up the early victories of the Arab Spring and engages scholars, activists, and journalists in a discussion of how (and

if) social networks fuel revolution. http://
english.aljazeera.net/programmes/emp
ire/2011/02/201121614532116986.html

- Visit Culturejammer Headquarters, http://www.
adbusters.org/, and see what Adbusters is about—
from videos to parody print advertisements. This is
where you can find the "Talking Rainforest" ad from
the late 1980s.

- Two more PBS Frontline documentaries: *Growing Up
Online* and *Digital Nation: Life on the Virtual Frontier*
offer insights on our changing media environment.

Advertising

People like dogs. People appreciate corporations that show social responsibility. Beer corporations want people—age 21 and over, of course—to purchase their products. Do the math and this adds up to a popular Super Bowl light beer commercial starring a mixed-breed rescue dog renamed Weego, an advertisement that illustrates contemporary branding trends.

The ad's setting is a party with friends. One man has recently adopted a dog from a shelter. The dog has a strange name. A partygoer calls the dog, "Here, Weego!" The dog fetches a light beer from the refrigerator. Cute, right? The last scene shows Weego, adorably scraggly, pushing a Styrofoam ice chest with text promoting a Facebook page. Corporate sponsors said the company would donate $1 (up to $250,000) to an animal rescue foundation for each "Like" the page received. People liked the page, the dog, and the company. Pop culture commentators applauded the beer company's melding of advertising, social networking, and promoting a useful cause.[2] "What better way to manage your corporate social responsibility strategy than to make a cute little rescued dog the face of your brand?[3]

The strategy reflects a creative solution to a contemporary problem. Branding experts note new ways of advertising are needed in an era of widespread distrust of corporations. Notes one trend-watching firm: "While 2011 saw new levels of consumer disgust at too many business' self-serving and often downright immoral (if not criminal) actions, stories of businesses doing good (Patagonia! Ben & Jerry's!) remind consumers that personality and profit can be compatible."[4]

Perhaps no force has shaped contemporary culture more than advertising. Ads are everywhere, lining our streets, filling our screens—and turning up in less likely places, including bathrooms, school buses, and doctor's offices. Young people are even invited to lease their bodies[5] as advertising space. Ad companies still try to reach people with traditional commercials at home and work when we're in front of our screens, but our eyeballs are also now sold to marketers when we're at school, sports events, or just goofing off.

"Consumers' viewing and reading habits are so scatter-shot now that many advertisers say the best way to reach time-pressed consumers is to try to catch their eye at literally every turn," writes Louise Story in a newspaper article aptly titled, "Anywhere the Eye Can See, It's Likely To See An Ad." A research firm calculates a person living 30 years ago in an urban environment saw around 2,000 ad messages a day. Today, we see about 5,000 ads daily.[6]

That kind of exposure to paid-for commercial speech is overwhelming to many. A PBS *Frontline* broadcast, "The Persuaders," explores the rise of commercialism in the

United States. Asked to respond to playwright Arthur Miller's assertion that "our culture now is advertising," author and professor Mark Crispin Miller noted a dismal shift in American values. He described what he sees as an unhealthy cynicism, a "snickering knee-jerk unbelief in any ideals whatsoever." Miller attributes this to the prevalence of an advertising culture that's now extended to a heavily commercialized political realm. "The all-but-total saturation of our culture by commercial advertising has surely helped intensify the general cynicism that we notice everywhere around us (and within us)," he argued.[7]

Miller also identifies another sort of "cynicism"—one that's realistic and skeptical—a "cynicism" that's not bored, powerless, and passive. That's the sort of cynicism that this book might describe as "criticism." A media critic doesn't need to throw up her hands and abdicate personal responsibility in the face of an ubiquitous advertising culture. We don't give up. A media critic looks carefully at the contemporary advertising realm and asks questions about its honesty, independence, and productivity. Awareness is the first step on the road to taking action. Hey, that might make a nice jingle.

And now for a word from our sponsors.

Advertising in 60 Seconds

For as long as people have been making and selling stuff, people have been advertising the stuff they make and sell. Think shopkeepers hollering in the streets of ancient Rome, giving away samples to entice new customers to buy.

Advertising, at its core, is a simple way to announce new products to people and persuade them to buy. In the early nineteenth century, U.S. newspapers and magazines contained advertisements for land sales, lodging, and transportation by train or stagecoach. Southern slave owners also placed newspaper ads offering rewards for runaway slaves.

Around the same time, factories began to produce goods, lots of goods. A problem soon emerged: products from one factory did not look much different from another factory's products. So, advertising was used to point out subtle (sometimes nonexistent) differences. This soap cleans better than the other soaps. This hair product makes your hair softer. This grain product tastes better.

Nowadays, advertising is considered one of several tools that help a company develop a deep connection with consumers. This is called "branding." It's not enough to convince people that one beverage tastes better than another. Companies seek to forge a new religion of sorts, a pseudo-spiritual feeling that consumers associate with a particular brand experience. Weego, the dog from the example at the start of this chapter, is not selling beer. He's selling a youthful lifestyle, punctuated by concern for animals, a lifestyle that would not be complete without Bud Light.

Is Advertising Honest?

Advertisers can't lie. That's the law. At least, in theory. In the United States, the Federal Trade Commission regulates advertising, which must be truthful and fair, not deceptive.

Advertisers are required to provide evidence to support any claims made in commercials. The rules for advertising are stiffer than the rules for pundits on cable TV news shows.

So, does sticking to the truth make advertising honest? Not exactly. Advertising is paid commercial speech with a goal—to sell a product, person, or idea. Providing an honest, well-rounded perspective about a product may not be as effective as creating a feel-good commercial that makes no real claims for which evidence might be required. A Coke commercial does not claim that drinking the beverage will bring world peace. Even though, in the ads, people of all races and cultures come together over an icy bottle of carbonated cola.

To understand how advertising can be truthful without necessarily being honest, we can look at some of the trade's tools. For decades, advertisers have relied on a few much-used persuasive techniques:

- **Celebrity endorsement.** These ads feature a famous person who lends her or his fame to the product being promoted. Examples: Actress Scarlett Johansson doing a SodaStream commercial, soccer star David Beckham hawking H&M undergarments, and actor and former California governor Arnold Schwarzenegger appearing in a Bud Light ad. Would the celebrity tout the product if he or she weren't being paid? If not, a celebrity endorsement is not honest.

- **Common folks approach.** These ads often show various settings with ordinary people whose lives are improved by the product. The Weego ad is an example. Average people are drinking this light beer. This is a beverage for everyone. Because no direct claims are being made, the common folks approach is more of a misdirection than an actual false claim.

- **Snob appeal.** We don't always want to be one of the common folks. Sometimes we want to feel like a rock star or an heiress. Ads selling luxury items from jewelry to expensive shoes to ocean cruises appeal to this feeling. The ads conflate the product with the desired emotion. That may not be lying but, as with the above technique, it's certainly manipulative.

- **Exploiting fears and insecurities.** Some advertisements offer a dismal, embarrassing anecdote followed by a remedy for what was concerning the person. A young man encounters attractive women who are disgusted when they see that he has dandruff or catch a whiff of his body odor. Buy the product. Attract the women. Again, this type of advertisement isn't a bald-faced lie. But hinting to consumers that the purchase of a product will solve social problems or get them a date? That's not exactly honest, either.

Chances are, you've seen ads that use the above techniques—and it's not hard to see through the persuasive strategy. Were we expecting commercials to give us undiluted truth about products that advertisers are trying to sell? Not usually.

Popular contemporary trends in advertising aren't any more honest than the see-through traditional methods. Advertisers in recent years have taken their art to a whole new level of subconscious appeal, using emotional branding to develop cult-like devotion to products being sold. Nike ads ooze messages of empowerment. The General Electric brand associates itself with innovation, "GE, we bring good things to life." People all over the world can "open happiness" with Coca-Cola.

Another recent trend employs honesty or at least the illusion of honesty in its branding campaign. The logic goes something like this: these days consumers are disillusioned with many corporations. Corporations seem greedy and unconcerned about the health of their employees, their customers, and the planet in general. A new breed of branding experts advise companies to create advertising messages that include a degree of transparency, a company admitting to its problems with its labor force or environmental record and showing consumers how it's working to solve these problems. "Consumers don't expect brands to be flawless. In fact, consumers will *embrace* brands . . . that are still brilliant despite having flaws," one trend-spotting agency proclaims. "Brands that show some empathy, generosity, humility, flexibility, maturity, humor, and (dare we say it) some character and humanity."[8]

One good example of how this plays out—the Coca-Cola Company, a company famous for its brilliant marketing efforts since the late 1800s. In recent years, Coca-Cola has been confronted by protests and boycotts for allegations of everything from contributing to childhood obesity to overuse of water in countries like India to connections to local murders of labor organizers at Coke bottling plants in South America.

How does a brand reclaim its reputation? The company trotted out its cartoon polar bears in 2011 for a campaign to save the Arctic habitat of real polar bears. Coke created white cans to advertise the company's efforts and to enlist the public's help in its benevolent social cause. A company that loves bears can't be that bad.

But Coke's feel-good campaign doesn't stop with bears. For Coke's "Open Happiness" campaign, the company filmed responses to a clever stunt. A Coke machine on college campuses dispensed free Cokes, pizzas, sunglasses—even flowers. Coke took a "special" truck to Rio de Janeiro, Brazil, and gave away Cokes, T-shirts, soccer balls—and a surfboard. "Where will happiness strike next?" reads the text atop the truck. Millions have watched the advertisements online. On YouTube, the spots end with an invitation to visit the company's Happiness Hub on Facebook. The ads give viewers a good feeling about the company as we see the company being benevolent to poor children on the streets of Rio.

That's how advertising has gotten away with not being quite honest—without directly lying. When pressed for a truthful answer to a hard question or to provide a well-rounded perspective about a product, skilled ad professionals change the debate. From its goals to its execution, advertising can't be honest. But is that what we expected it to be? Probably not.

Is Advertising Independent?

From the start, the nature of the advertising beast seems to have been one that's less than independent. A commercial selling a pain reliever will probably not include interviews or a spreadsheet that fairly compares and contrasts the benefits and side effects of all pain relievers. We expect a bias from advertisers—a bias in favor of the product, person, or idea being promoted.

What we perhaps don't consider, however, is the extent to which advertisers control the information in a country like the United States, where most mass media are private businesses—and many rely on advertising to pay many or all of the bills. Because of the for-profit nature of media industries, commercial sponsors have a great amount of power. In his book, *AdCult USA*, James B. Twitchell notes the irony that the First Amendment of the U.S. Constitution guarantees press freedom from government interference but not from external corporate forces—or from sources within the media that must pander to the external corporate forces. "As a general rule, the greater the advertising load, the greater the sponsor's control of content," Twitchell wrote. "He who pays the piper calls the tune. What needs inspection is not why the media favors advertising interests, but why we are so shocked at the collusion."[9]

Perhaps Twitchell's question is best answered by the media critic who understands how corporate advertisers use their great power over media to mask that power, to make us trust the company and the product, to make us feel better about ourselves and our world. Corporate profits depend on consumers not looking, like Dorothy in *The Wizard of Oz*, behind the curtain to discover the real nature of the wizard.

Examples of how corporations use advertising dollars to control media content abound. Many stunning examples come from the tobacco industry, which spent decades trying to convince people to keep smoking—even as smokers were dropping like flies from lung cancer.

Twitchell quotes a university research team that studied 100 magazines for 20 years and found that magazines that ran tobacco ads were 38 percent less likely to run stories about the risks of tobacco. Even magazines that promoted good health were guilty. *Cosmopolitan* magazine editor Helen Gurley Brown famously explained to a reporter, "Having come from the advertising world myself, I think, 'Who needs someone you're paying millions of dollars a year to come back and bite you on the ankle?'" [10]

In 1957, the American Tobacco Company punished *Reader's Digest* for running an article warning of the dangers of cigarette smoking. The tobacco company convinced its advertising agency to stop working with *Reader's Digest*, costing the magazine $1.6 million. In the 1980s, the nation's largest tobacco companies acquired new family-friendly brands that extended the tobacco companies' control. RJR Reynolds, makers of Camel cigarettes and other brands, bought Nabisco—complete with the Keebler elves. Phillip Morris, maker of Marlboro and other brands, bought Kraft and its snack products. Those acquisitions helped the tobacco companies control media sources that didn't run tobacco ads—but that did run ads for cookies and cream cheese. *Reader's Digest* learned its lesson from the 1950s. In 1986, the magazine refused to print the American Heart Association's supplement on links between heart disease and cigarette smoking. [11]

Then again, returning to the question of independence, it's worth noting that the advertising companies themselves are not independent. They collect paychecks from their corporate employers—and can be disciplined, just like a magazine or newspaper. In 1988, the newly merged food and tobacco company RJR Nabisco Inc. flexed its muscles and fired its longtime advertising agency. Why? The agency had, for another client, announced the nation's first smoking ban on airplanes.[12] Ad company Saatchi & Saatchi lost an ad contract worth between $70 and $80 million for creating an ad that shows folks packed on a plane. Several passengers are smoking. When the ban is announced, the rest of the passengers on the plane stand up and applaud.

Twitchell's first rule of *Adcult*? "Speech is never free."[13] What does that mean for advertising's independence? The folks able to pay for commercial messages have the most independence (least regulation) over the content of their speech. Those who rely on advertising dollars to pay the bills have the least independence. Caught in the middle are the advertising agencies themselves, which may end up trying to mediate conflicting goals of different clients.

Is Advertising Productive?

Advertising is an effective means of persuasion. The global effectiveness of advertising tobacco products, for example, worries antismoking advocates at the World Health Organization. Whether the advertising is directly placed on a billboard or indirectly placed through sponsorship of, say, a rock concert or a sports event, tobacco advertising succeeds in associating cigarette smoking "with athletic prowess, sexual attractiveness, professional success, adult sophistication, independence, adventure and self-fulfillment," according to a WHO report.[14] From an industry standpoint, this is a triumph in branding. But WHO sees it differently. "This constant barrage of misleading messages appeals to young people and encourages them to take up a behavior harmful to their health."[15] The report cited an "overwhelming majority of independent, peer-reviewed studies" linking tobacco advertising to the habits and attitudes of young people, also known as "replacement smokers." That's right, replacement smokers.

Tobacco companies need young people to start smoking because the adult smokers are dying from heart disease and lung cancer. Advertising regulation in the United States, including a ban on TV commercials, has forced tobacco companies to find innovative ways of making their product look cool. And global markets offer vast new supplies of replacement smokers in countries where tobacco products and advertising are less regulated.

Does advertising work? Of course. It sells its products. But in our introductory chapter, we used Jonas Salk's quote as a gauge for productivity. Does advertising make us better ancestors? An advocacy group, Children Now, notes that companies spend $15 billion a year creating advertising that directly targets children under the age of 12. That amount has doubled in the past decade. The younger a child is, the more susceptible to ad messages. Most children under age 8 can't sort commercials from the rest of programming and tend to accept advertising as accurate or unbiased. Branding works, even with toddlers. A 30-second commercial can influence brand preferences in children as young as 2 years.[16]

Let's return to the Weego beer ad and consider its impact on children. The ad certainly does not target children directly. Yet, the ad ran during the Super Bowl, a family-friendly event. A 2010 study on measuring youth exposure to alcohol advertising cites 13 studies linking underage youth exposure to alcohol advertising and underage drinking.[17] That's a problem, given that nearly one-third of young people age 12 to 20 reported drinking in a National Survey on Drug Use and Health. Around 7.2 million young people reported frequent binge drinking (five or more drinks in one session). Underage drinking is responsible for 5,000 deaths annually of people under age 21. Underage drinking costs society tens of billions in a given year, according to the study.[18] If this is beginning to sound preachy, it's because mass media have taught us to view tobacco and alcohol consumption as a right, a rebellion, a cool thing to do.

On the plus side, because advertising is effective, it can be used to convince people to change bad habits, as did a 2012 U.S. government-funded national advertising campaign—"Tips from Former Smokers." One advertisement in the series begins with a photo of a youthful woman and a raspy voice-over: "I'm Terrie and I used to be a smoker." The image shifts to Terrie now, providing tips on how to get ready for a day. For Terrie, that means inserting her dentures, putting on her wig, installing her hands-free device over the stoma, or hole, in her throat—so that she can talk with her voice prosthesis. The tone of the ad is straightforward. The content is emotionally wrenching. The ad is one of several in the "Tips from Former Smokers" series conducted by the U.S. Centers for Disease Control and Prevention. The campaign is credited with prompting 1.6 million smokers to try to quit smoking. More than 100,000 succeeded, according to a government-funded study.[19]

Advertising funded by the government can be used to persuade people in useful ways. But what about private companies? Feeling under attack by those who doubt that advertising can be, overall, a productive tool in a democratic society, Ed Gillespie, founder of Futerra Sustainability Communications, responded with examples of companies creating useful ad campaigns. One such campaign is for Peugot's MU, a car company's "mobility service" that rents bikes, electric cars, and other vehicles in some cities. The Peugot's ads focus on "intrinsic values of affiliation, self-acceptance, community, benevolence and universalism" and the campaign not only buoys a new market but also encourages "aggregate, but collaborative, consumption" in a sustainable way. That's a good campaign, Gillespie argued.[20] Gillespie agreed that advertising has permeated our culture and created a jaded populace. He said advertising directed to children could be banned without too much protest from thinking people. Most interesting to the media critic might be his quoting of a Greenpeace activist on the topic of advertising: "Creative communication is like a kitchen knife—you can use it to prepare a beautiful, delicious meal. Or you can use it to stab your wife."[21]

Productive? Not in alcohol and tobacco advertising and ads directed at children. But hearty approval to antismoking campaigns and commercials that encourage people to live more sustainably. Yes, it's a mixed bag—advertising.

BE THE CRITIC

The advertising of U.S. political candidates on television began in the 1950s and forever changed the way campaigns would be run.

- Visit the Living Room Candidate's archive of political campaign commercials 1952–2008, http://www. livingroomcandidate.org. Choose three presidential campaigns from three different decades to compare and contrast.

- Watch the advertisements carefully. Take notes, describing the details of the commercial.

- Ask questions: What's the topic of the ad? What kind of music, jingles, or soundtracks are used? What kinds of images are shown? Can you identify the persuasive technique at work?

- Identify patterns. What do the ads have in common? How many ads promote the positive attributes of a candidate, and how many attack an opponent? How have advertising techniques changed over the decades?

- Evaluate the effectiveness of the ads. What's working for you? Why?

SATIATE YOUR CURIOSITY

- Visit Adbusters.org, Culture Jammer headquarters, to keep track of the latest in media literacy activism. http://www.adbusters.org

- *PBS Frontline* offers ad-themed documentaries in streaming form at the show's website. "Merchants of Cool" (2000) follows the efforts of Viacom's MTV and cool-hunting trend spotters to market to teenagers; "The Persuaders" (2004) offers an insightful exploration of contemporary methods employed by the advertising and public relations industries.

- Movies are reviewed weekly for their unpaid tobacco company product placement at SceneSmoking.org. http://www.scenesmoking.org

- Naomi Klein's book *No Logo* (1999) examines corporate branding efforts and contemporary social movements that break down advertising messages and build media literacy.

Public Relations

"Public relations is a real benign-sounding term to describe propaganda."

—John Stauber, PR Watch[1]

More than 200 years ago, an activist group in the American colonies of Great Britain illegally boarded ships in the Boston harbor. Wearing disguises, the men dumped hundreds of chests of imported tea into the water. Why? To protest a British taxation policy. The Boston Tea Party was called the "greatest and best known publicity stunt of all time" by *PRWeek*.[2] Its target audience was both the British government and the colonists.

Flash forward more than 200 years to a public event in 2012 during which animal rights activists threw white flour at Kim Kardashian. Why? Kardashian wears real fur coats and sports $5,000 boots made from python skins. While the publicity stunt didn't exactly make front-page news, the story was covered on gossip websites, Entertainment Tonight, VH1, and the *Washington Post*'s Celebritology blog.[3] Although the act was much smaller in scale than the Boston Tea Party, this event was planned to accomplish a similar purpose—to shift public opinion, in this case about clothing made from animal skins.

Whether a political group stages a historic protest like the Boston Tea Party or eco-activists fling flour, the action is designed to get the public's attention. The publicity stunt, also called a "pseudo-event," is one of many public relations strategies with some deep roots in the United States.

What's public relations? How does it differ from advertising and marketing? The term *public relations* describes using a wide range communication tools to strategically influence public thought and build goodwill on behalf of a person, business, political party, or ideology. A public relations campaign might include paid advertising as one part of a much broader approach. But strategists more often look for ways to get a message out to large numbers of people without buying space for a company's message on a billboard or placing a website banner. For decades, that required generating news coverage in print and broadcast media. Today, that might mean making a popular YouTube video that ends up watched by millions—and also gets covered by print, broadcast, and online news media. Then and now, public relations practitioners are expert at crafting a message and getting it in front of the right people in any media platform.

Crafting a message begins with research—gathering information about an issue, individual, group, or organization and analyzing this data to determine what type of communication problems might exist with a given audience. Public relations practitioners form a plan to solve this problem. They consider what their audience needs to see and hear in order to improve relations with the client. Then, these strategic communicators decide how best to spread that message, whether through a social media campaign, a press release that gains news media coverage, a pseudo-event, or sending out a direct mailing to homes and businesses. Finally, the public relations strategists evaluate their work. Was the audience reached with the message? What was the reaction or effect?

A public relations firm might be hired by a small business, a large corporation, a famous or wealthy individual, a government agency, or even an entire nation. Long before being ousted in an uprising led by the National Transitional Council in 2011, Libyan dictator Muammar Gaddafi hired an international public relations company to improve his regime's image. The firm Brown Lloyd James advised Gaddafi and other Libyan leaders about how to mold international opinion to support them. Public relations experts from the company arranged interviews between journalists and Gaddafi. The firm edited opinion columns written by the leader and submitted these writings to newspapers and websites.[4] The controversial leader paid the PR firm millions.

Activist or social reform advocates use public relations strategies as well. A staged or pseudo-event might be one strategy that activists use to gain media attention, those front-page stories or lead TV news bits. Occupy Wall Street was one example of how a group of people can inject conversations into the media without having to resort to paid advertising. Occupy Wall Street received plenty of media attention, some of it negative. Nonetheless, it succeeded in introducing one of its main messages or talking points—that 99 percent of a nation's population may not be well-served by lawmakers whose election and governing decisions are influenced by the donations of a wealthy minority.

PR practitioners who work directly for a government agency, business, or politician can hold press conferences with reporters, carefully communicating a story that shows their client in the best possible light. Print and video press releases—news stories written to make their subject look good—are issued to news media sources, who may run the stories on websites or broadcast them without noting that these "stories" were not reported by journalists.

A public relations professional considers her work well done when she sees key ideas or even the exact wording from a news conference or press release on an important newspaper's website or when she sees her video news release running unedited on the evening news. The agency or business did not pay for the story to be written; as already noted, this isn't advertising. No money changed hands between the agency or business and the news media. Yet, there's a front-page story making the agency or business look good. What could be better than that? Even the hard-working journalist is pleased. Having a complete story handed to the reporter means a little less work on deadline.

In fact, as newsrooms shrink, more journalists rely on information in press releases to fuel their stories in print, online, and broadcast. By some estimates, public relations efforts make up almost half of the information that individuals see, hear, and read in the news media. In *Trust Us, We're Experts,* a book that probes public relations practices, Sheldon Rampton and John Stauber note that, in a typical issue of *The Wall Street Journal,* more than half the news stories came from press releases. They quote a study in the *Columbia Journalism Review,* which wrote that the stories were often taken word for word from the press release, "with little additional reporting." Many of these articles appeared to the reader to be written "by a *Wall Street Journal* reporter."[5] The public reads and views this information as news. The actual source of the story is invisible to the reader.

Analyzing public relations messages is critical, argue the journalists, because of PR's impact on democracy in countries like the United States. A group, PR Watch, was established by the Center for Media and Democracy to act as a journalistic "watchdog" over the propaganda industries. PR Watch investigated the influence of public relations over major events, including the 2012 presidential campaign and election in the United States—noting that more money was spent to influence this "than ever before in the history of the world."[6]

PR Watch pays particular attention to so-called citizen groups that spend millions of dollars on political advertising to support a candidate aligned with their interests. As a result of the Supreme Court's 2010 *Citizens United* decision, in which the Court ruled that the government couldn't restrict political spending by corporations or labor unions, these large organizations are allowed to spend gobs of money to influence the political process. Funds are channeled to political action committees or PACs with vague names like Restore Our Future, a super-PAC that supported the Republican presidential candidate in 2012.[7]

A smart media critic works to understand the role of public relations in U.S. and global media. Whether we come upon a website or social media post or encounter more traditional news media that seem to promote a political party or a large corporation's perspective, we need to ask some questions. Is this a public relations effort? As such, is it honest, independent, and productive?

Is Public Relations Honest?

In the 1800s, some individuals and organizations in the United States hired press agents to make the public pay attention to them. Press agents made American heroes and legends out of the likes of Davy Crockett, Daniel Boone, and Annie Oakley, a female sharpshooter who drew crowds of paying customers to *Buffalo Bill's Wild West Show*. To draw folks to such shows as Buffalo Bill's or to traveling circuses like those of P. T. Barnum, press agents would send out press releases full of exaggerations and sometimes lies. Newspaper reporters would be bribed with free tickets to the show. Today, public relations practitioners try to distance themselves from the checkered past of the 1800s press agent and counter the stigma still attached to public relations as a less-than-honest profession.

One pioneer of contemporary public relations was Ivy Ledbetter Lee, who believed that companies should let the media know what was going on in their businesses. Lee argued for transparency and openness—but he wasn't above shaping that "transparent" message into one that made his clients come out looking squeaky clean. One of his clients was the wealthy Rockefeller family. They had been blamed for the Ludlow Massacre of 1914 in which the Colorado National Guard and camp guards attacked striking miners, setting fire to the workers' homes, killing workers, 2 women, and 11 children. The Rockefellers, who held a controlling interest in the company that owned the mine, hired Lee to repair their public image. Lee advised John D. Rockefeller, Jr. to visit the mining camps to talk to miners and their families. He invited reporters and photographers to write about and take pictures of Rockefeller swinging a pickax in the mines and having a beer with the miners after the day's work was done.

"The press loved it . . . Rockefeller was portrayed as being seriously concerned about the plight of workers, and the visit led to policy changes and more worker benefits."[8] Was this a well-rounded portrayal of a wealthy business owner who cared about his employees? Hardly. Was it a lie? No, it wasn't that either. Lee's advice to Rockefeller led to better relations between the Rockefeller family and the U.S. public, and some good came for the workers as well. Manipulating public opinion lacks transparency. That's the opposite of honest.

Nowadays, a public relations campaign uses a variety of means to expose the public to its carefully crafted message. It might put the message in the mouths of trusted sources on radio talk shows or cable TV. It might create a Facebook page or an advocacy website. Like advertising, the carefully crafted message may be truthful. Every factual detail might check out. But if the message doesn't contain a full range of information, if some details are left out, it can't be considered honest. If the public sees only the Rockefeller who stands beside his workers in the mines—and not the Rockefeller who hires men to attack strikers, the public is not seeing the whole picture.

Let's take a close look at honesty in a more recent award-winning public relations campaign from the early 2000s. First, the problem. People weren't using as much paper. Between environmental awareness campaigns that started in the 1970s and the computer revolution during the 1990s and the first decade of the new century, the U.S. public had decreased its use of paper so much that the wood and paper industries were feeling the pain of falling profits. In 2005–2006, several logging and paper companies banded together to hire the public relations agency Porter Novelli. The agency researched the problem and came up with a plan of action for this group of companies, now dubbed the "Abundant Forests Alliance" (AFA). The name of the group itself is part of a strategy to convince the public that forests are not endangered by the paper industry. In fact, forests are "abundant." America has no shortage of trees, at all, the agency argues simply by using the word *alliance* in the name of this group—doubtless a coalition of genial businesses working together for (what sounds like) a positive goal.

Porter Novelli devised a $10 million campaign called "Renew, Reuse, and Respect," targeting college-educated women, nicknamed "legacy moms,"[9] who had kids living at home. The campaign's goal was to make these women feel better about the forestry and paper industries. Strategies included the publication of a kid's book, *The Tree Farmer,* written by Chuck Leavell, Rolling Stones keyboardist and tree farmer. Leavell promoted his book on websites, TV talk shows, and magazine articles—all media that legacy moms watch and read. To further accelerate good feelings about paper, Porter Novelli hired celebrities to endorse gift ideas made from paper. Women were encouraged to start scrapbooks at free demonstrations in 500 Walmart stores across the nation. The campaign was considered a success, based on the number of people who engaged with the Abundant Forest Alliance's messages and on surveys that showed "improved public perceptions and the state of forests in North America."[10] *PRWeek* named it the Public Affairs Campaign of the Year in 2007.[11]

So, was the campaign honest? The campaign informed its audience that 750 million acres of forestland exist in the United States and that that amount hadn't changed much in a century.[12] The U.S. Forest Service confirms that

750 million acres of forestland exist, and that when the Service was established in 1905, the amount was 760 million acres.[13] But the U.S. Department of the Interior puts this number in context, explaining that between the mid-1600s and the early twentieth century, about 300 million acres of forest were cleared.[14] That number adds to our understanding of U.S. forestlands but it's not highlighted in the AFA campaign. The campaign isn't lying—but it is directing our attention to the facts that make us feel OK about using paper. It's distracting us from other facts that don't contribute to that goal.

An honest and transparent campaign might also have made consumers aware of the companies who are members of the Abundant Forests Alliance[15] and their environmental records. What kinds of companies were behind the children's book and the scrapbooking workshops? The campaign made no mention of toxic waste dumped at dozens of sites in the United States and around the world by these industries. One Alliance member, International Paper, one of the world's largest forest products company, is listed by the Environmental Protection Agency as the responsible party on contaminated Superfund sites[16] in several states including Minnesota,[17] Michigan,[18] and New Jersey.[19] Another member, MeadWestvaco, is a global packaging solutions company held partly responsible by the Environmental Protection Agency for dumping a million tons of toxic waste at a landfill in Virginia during the 1980s.[20]

On the bright side, these days it's getting harder for public relations practitioners to control certain types of information. Thanks to consumer and political watchdog websites and databases accessible online, the public no longer has to rely on information that may be filtered by strategic communicators. Thus the tactics of public relations professionals have had to shift in ways that might be seen as increasingly honest. "Radical forms of transparency are now the norm at start-ups—and even some Fortune 500 companies," reports Clive Thompson in *Wired* magazine. "Now firms spill information in torrents, posting internal memos and strategy goals, letting everyone from the top dog to shop-floor workers blog publicly about what their firm is doing right—and wrong."[21]

This is great, right? Tons of information. Everything you'd want to know about an individual, company, political party, organization, or idea is all right there, waiting for us to find it. Now, we just need to learn how to look. That's the goal of becoming media literate.

The public's looking forward to a time when strategic communications operates with complete transparency. For failing to reveal all the facts and all the allegiances all the time, public relations earns a low score for its honesty.

Are Public Relations Campaigns Independent?

This is a simple question, simple answer: No. The point of a public relations campaign is to create persuasive media on behalf of a company, individual, political party, religious organization, issue, or idea. If the message is independent, it's art—and thus not public relations. To clarify, let's look at the story of two books about the environmental consequences of the logging industry. One is Dr. Seuss's famous book *The Lorax* (1971); the other is *The*

Truax (1995), a parody of Seuss's book sponsored by the hardwood flooring industry.

Seuss had been a propagandist during World War II. But he wasn't operating as a member of any environmental group when he wrote *The Lorax*. He wasn't paid to create a message that would convince young people to protect forests. He created an artful book, independent of any agenda other than his own philosophical leanings.

Seuss's book was not an attack on forestry practices or companies that harvested wood from forests in sustainable ways, taking selected large trees but leaving a diversity of plants and trees to grow. It was directed at what were arguably more ecologically destructive logging practices.

Seuss's book wasn't well-received by logging companies and the paper industry. The National Wood Flooring Manufacturers' Association (NOFMA) Environmental Committee paid mother of two and "active member of the hardwood flooring industry" Terri Birkett to write a rhyming book that showed the industry in a more favorable light.[22] In Birkett's book, *The Truax*, a cranky creature called "the Guardbark" is initially unwilling to listen to reason. But in the end, the Guardback becomes convinced that the lumber industry plants more trees than it chops down and is the best friend of biodiversity.

On endangered species? "Would anyone mind if we lost, say, a tick—that carried a germ that made cuddlebears sick? Or what about something that's really quite nice? Like the yellow-striped minnow that lives in Lake Zice? How far will we go and how much will we pay to keep a few minnows from dying away?"[23] The rhyming language repeats an industry message of that era—jobs for humans are more important than the habitat for endangered species. To its credit, NOFMA was completely transparent with the publication of *The Truax*. The book's last page credits the author, lists her biography, and explains that NOFMA is comprised of hardwood flooring manufacturers. This message was honest—honest about being less than independent of bias.

The 2012 release of the movie *The Lorax* became a tool for political controversy. Fox Business host Lou Dobbs pointed to "liberal" plotlines in *The Lorax*, claiming such movies are intended to indoctrinate young people with subversive anticapitalist messages. "The president's liberal friends in Hollywood [are] targeting a younger demographic using animated movies to sell their agenda to children," Dobbs said.[24] Another journalist interviewed Seuss's widow, asking if the book—and the movie—was an indoctrination attempt. "I think any and all talk about the environment cannot be written off as propaganda," offered Audrey Stone Geisel, Seuss's widow, arguing for independent thought in art.[25]

A children's book like that of Dr. Seuss can be considered independent—even if it has a message that seems biased to critics. No one paid Seuss to take the stand that he took. A children's book that's funded by a for-profit industry and written to improve the industry's image is a public relations tactic. Public relations is, by its nature, not independent.

Are Public Relations Campaigns Productive?

April 2010. The oil-drilling rig *Deepwater Horizon*, exploded in the Gulf of Mexico. Eleven workers were killed. Millions of gallons of oil gushed into the Gulf of Mexico, killing shrimp, fish, turtles, dolphins, birds, and other marine life. Oil washed up on beaches and wetlands, killing wildlife, plants—and the Gulf Coast tourism industry. For three months, oil poured into the ocean before workers could cap the well six miles under the ocean's surface. For *Deepwater Horizon's* owner BP, a London-based oil company with a global reach, the disaster wasn't merely environmental. The company's reputation was taking a huge hit. While oil was still flowing into the Gulf, the company kicked off an intense public relations campaign to help manage BP's image crisis. By some accounts, BP was spending $5 million per week running advertisements in newspapers and magazines and on television.[26] Can we say this was productive? Critics suggested that the money could have been better spent. "While BP's advertising campaign ramped up, businesses and the Gulf communities struggled to deal with the costs of the disaster," U.S. Rep. Kathy Castor said.[27]

A specialized branch of public relations devotes itself to crisis communication, a field that concentrates on salvaging the reputations of companies or public figures who've provoked the public ire. These crises might include Prince Harry's nude photos in Las Vegas, quarterback Michael Vick's dog-fighting ring, or the infamous image of Olympic swimmer Michael Phelps smoking pot. A well-executed public relations plan can help a company or person regain public favor. But does that make the offending entity—or the dissuaded public—better ancestors? Perhaps it does, if the public relations campaign involves the person or entity taking responsibility for the actions and making amends.

Crisis communications can be useful during larger tragic events—terrorist attacks, war, disease outbreaks, natural disasters, oil spills, etc.—that affect a much wider swath of people. A well-executed crisis management plan can be a productive means of getting information to the public in such dire situations.

Yet, while strategic communications tools can help a multinational corporation with an image crisis, they also are used by organizations with humanitarian goals—for example, Doctors Without Borders (Médecins Sans Frontières [MSF]), a French organization that offers medical care to people involved in violent conflicts in places like Africa. Because MSF takes no political stand in a conflict, its medical staff usually is allowed to travel with fewer barriers. The goal of MSF's strategic communication efforts is "to increase awareness of human rights abuses or neglected crises . . . it tries to act as a witness."[28] To accomplish this, MSF maintains a website, a Twitter account, a Facebook page, and a presence on other social media like LinkedIn. The nongovernmental organization also sends out press releases, hires individuals to talk to and convince (lobby) lawmakers who might improve human rights policies, and places articles in magazines about its work. It regularly sends out pleas for donations via direct mail. The ability of MSF to do its work depends on its receiving support from governments and people in the places it works and also on donations from individuals, foundations, and businesses. Without public relations strategies and practices, humanitarian organizations like MSF, Oxfam, Save the Children Fund, and World Vision would be crippled.

Persuasive tools are, after all, simply tools. They can be used to help feed starving children around the globe. They can be used to keep people feeling good about the company responsible for the largest oil spill in history. Which makes us better ancestors?

BE THE CRITIC

- Create a list of causes worthy of a publicity campaign. Choose one that might represent your effort to be a better ancestor.

- Consider your audience. Who will you target with your campaign?

- Plan your message. It should be something simple. Remember "Give a hoot, don't pollute" or "just say no" to drugs? Those are memorable.

- Plan a pseudo-event, publicity stunt, or press conference to attract a media audience.

- Create buzz through printed posters and handouts—and through social networking. You want to get people interested in your event so that the media will be interested in your event.

- Hold your event. Take pictures. Post 'em to Facebook to spread the message some more. If a newspaper reporter or television station shows up, you win big! Congratulations.

SATIATE YOUR CURIOSITY

- The movie *Thank You for Smoking* offers a funny, insightful glimpse into the life of a fictional PR representative for tobacco companies.

- Check out BP's YouTube channel and consider the message the company is delivering through social media. http://www.youtube.com/bp#p/u/1/vbqjOiCJEGM

- While you're at it, visit BP's Team USA page on Facebook. It's created for the paralympic athletic team that competed in the 2012 Special Olympics. http://www.facebook.com/BPTeamUSA?ref=ts

- Now, take a look at Democracy Now's coverage of the BP oil spill. http://www.democracynow.org/topics/bp_oil_spill

 **Reality TV**

"[American] Idol reveals so much about American thinking—
about hopes and dreams, about business and the packaging
of human beings, about gamesmanship and rivalry and des-
peration, about judgment, about what attracts us and repels
us in each other, about joy and sorrow and this point in history
at which raw emotion is captured on camera and on stage."

—Anneli Rufus, "American Idol Is a Mind
Game," *Psychology Today*, March 4, 2009

Like all the amateur performers who came to auditions
in Galveston, Texas, and other U.S. locations, Phong Vu
wanted to be the next American Idol. "It feels so good
inside to have something big [*sic*] achievement," he said
in an interview, through tears. "It's so phenomenon [*sic*].
It's amazing." Vu faced the *Idol* judges with confidence
and sang Toni Braxton's "Unbreak My Heart"—an off-key,
melody-free version. At the end of his short performance,
Idol judge Jennifer Lopez tried not to laugh out loud. She
delivered the bad news. "It's not going to work this time
but thank you, sweetie," Lopez said. Vu shed tears and
promised to be back next year. Nearly 20 million tuned
in to watch the Galveston auditions on TV. Hundreds of
thousands watched audition video clips at the *American
Idol* website and on YouTube.

American Idol and other reality TV shows rely on unscripted scenes and dialogue from "real" people, who are carefully selected from huge pools of fame-seeking candidates. Programs have tapped the talents of ordinary folks since the radio quiz shows of the 1930s and Allen Funt's *Candid Microphone* in 1948. In 1973, a 12-episode documentary series, *An American Family,* aired on PBS. Often considered the first reality TV show, the series documented an American family, the Louds, during a year that included a gay son's public coming out and the separation and eventual divorce of parents Bill and Pat Loud. Anthropologist Margaret Mead called the show's form "as new and significant as the invention of drama or the novel."[1]

Reality TV has long been a hit with TV companies, providing content on a tight budget, and also with audiences, who may, scholars suggest, be attracted to amateur performances out of a desire to validate their own existence through media status. Even after TV had been around for decades, "places in the broadcast circus were still reserved for 'real people,'" writes Todd Gitlin in his book, *Media Unlimited.*[2] Over the years, amateurs have competed in talent contests (*American Idol*) or submitted silly recordings of family mishaps (*America's Funniest Home Videos*)." People who watch TV, Gitlin writes, are no longer satisfied with merely being fans of its content. We fantasize about being on other side of the screen. "Reality TV allows Americans to fantasize about gaining status through automatic fame," write Dr. Steven Reiss and James Wiltz in a *Psychology Today* article. "Ordinary people can watch the shows, see people like themselves and imagine that they too could become celebrities by being on television. It does not matter as much that the contestants often are shown in an unfavorable light; the fact that millions of

Americans are paying attention means that the contestants are important."[3] Hopeful superstar Phong Vu sang off-key on *American Idol* to get his few minutes of fame.

For large media businesses, the money-making potential of reality TV became obvious when 51 million people tuned in to watch the finale of *Survivor*'s first season in 2000. The profit formula continues to work. Because makers of reality TV shows don't pay professional writers or actors, the shows can be produced for much less than a scripted episode of, say, *Modern Family* or *Mad Men*. In addition, plenty of money can be made from product placement and brand integration. Advertisers appreciate millions of viewers seeing their commercials or viewing products placed deliberately in the shows themselves. Reality TV is a money-making machine for media corporations.

Profitability and popularity combined explain the profusion of reality TV shows and spin-offs on all networks. Although *Survivor*'s ratings eventually plummeted, other reality shows rose to take its place. Audiences can watch chefs compete, teen moms cope, men swap wives, cops chase sex predators, and family members hold "interventions" for loved ones with drug problems. Community college drop-out Nicole "Snooki" Polizzi became a celebrity on what seemed to be an endless reality drinking binge in MTV's *Jersey Shore* that continued on *Snooki & JWOWW*. *American Idol* held top spots on the Nielsen Top Ten charts for broadcast television for nearly a decade before losing some of its audience to *The Voice* and *Dancing with the Stars*.[4] *American Idol* had been the most-watched show for adults between the ages of 18 and 49 for eight seasons through 2012. In 2011, the show was nominated for 10 prime-time Emmy Awards—from Outstanding

Reality-Competition Program to Outstanding Host for Ryan Seacrest.[5]

Audiences like reality television. Media corporations profit from it. So why do some people scorn reality TV programming while others feign embarrassment for an obsession with it? In 2011, a controversial question on some SAT exams[6] asked about the merits of reality television. American teenagers were required to formulate a response to the question: "Do people benefit from forms of entertainment that show so-called reality, or are such forms of entertainment harmful?" Outrage ensued. Were the writers of SAT essay questions assuming young people should take time away from studying physics, chemistry, and foreign languages to watch mindless women compete on *The Bachelor*? Was this a sign that the SAT exams were becoming less high-brow along with the rest of popular culture? Surely cultural anarchy loomed, critics feared.

A cynic might be quick to dismiss reality television as proof of social decay, evidence that media scholar Neil Postman was correct when he observed that shallow TV entertainment has replaced substantive discussion of topics important in a society like ours. "Our politics, religion, news, athletics, education, and commerce have been transformed into congenial adjuncts of show business," Postman writes, "largely without protest or even much popular notice. The result is that we are a people on the verge of amusing ourselves to death."[7] That sounds dismal. And, Postman wasn't even referring directly to reality TV. But a critic takes a closer look at how audiences use reality television as entertainment and even as an information source. True, at the end of a programming day, a critic might conclude that some reality shows are useless drivel. But, the critic gives the medium a chance before deeming the entire genre without value. The critic watches shows like *Duck Dynasty* while asking questions about reality television's honesty, its independence, and its productive role as social discourse.

Is Reality Television Honest?

To look at honesty in reality TV, a critic might travel in time back to the medium's start, when many considered television to be a trusted source of information. In the mid-1950s, television was still a new phenomenon for American families. The popular reality TV of that era included quiz shows that drew huge audiences. Viewers enjoyed watching regular people like themselves have a chance to win huge sums of money on CBS shows like *The $64,000 Question* or *Twenty-One*, on which a contestant could win as much as a quarter-million dollars.

Before long, a problem emerged. Viewers discovered the quiz shows were rigged—the show's directors manipulated the contestants, the questions, and, ultimately, the winner. Congressional hearings were held to investigate the quiz show scandals. *Twenty-One* and *The $64,000 Question* went off the air. The viewing public was heart-broken and disillusioned. For a while. If a quiz show with real-life contestants wasn't honest, could people trust anything on television? TV critic Steven Stark writes that the scandals led to a lasting cynicism about the media in the United States. "The revelation that some of these popular shows had been rigged shocked America, causing a national reappraisal not only of that new phenomenon, television, but also of that older one, the American character."[8] The scandals rocked our national identity. But, before long, U.S.

audiences came to terms with TV's fictions. As it turned out, viewers missed the drama of reality media. A PBS documentary about the quiz show scandals cites a *Miami Herald* poll that found readers were not outraged by the hoaxes: "Most Miamians wanted the shows back, regardless of all that had taken place. 'Everything on TV is somewhat of a lie,' one viewer explained to the *Herald*, 'but it's still entertainment.'"[9] Americans were willing to suspend disbelief and watch quiz show heroes rise and fall, Stark writes. As a result, Americans watched more TV, not less.[10] It seemed that honesty simply didn't matter so much.

Today, reality TV shows screen participants for their ability to do well on the show and to appeal to the viewing public. We're fully aware that the "regular" people we see on reality TV have been primped, coached, and, at times, psychologically primed for intense drama. Audiences expect this now. We've even heard dark stories about torturous experiences of participants. In recent years, reports from former contestants on shows such as *The Bachelor* suggest that some reality TV production crews have kept contestants cloistered from the comforts of friends, family, and technology, subjected to gruelingly long filming days, and encouraged to drink excessive amounts of alcohol to encourage reckless actions.

One former contestant talked to the *New York Times* about her experience on ABC's show *The Bachelor* in 2006. Contestants waited in vans for hours. Parties included little food but plenty of wine. "When producers judged the proceedings too boring, they sent out a production assistant with a tray of shots. 'If you combine no sleep with alcohol and no food, emotions are going to run high and people are going to be acting crazy,' said Erica Rose, a contestant that year."[11] Rose was one of two dozen former contestants who spoke to the *Times* reporter. Most contestants told stories that revealed a pattern of "isolation, sleeplessness, and alcohol to encourage wild behavior." Reality wasn't exciting enough on its own, so producers helped make things more dramatic. That type of manipulation is anything but honest.

In addition to manufacturing an arguably unreal environment for contestants, recorded video footage is carefully edited to highlight dramas and sensationalize conflict. Mundane moments are dismissed. Boring! The footage aired is memorable, crazy, attention-getting. The result? A high-pitched, action-packed "reality." The constant intensity of this fake reality can't possibly be matched by our own authentic (boring) experience. The drama rivets us to our screens.

As in the aftermath of the quiz show scandals, reality TV audiences today also don't expect authenticity from their media experiences. When viewers were polled by the Associated Press about the truthfulness of reality shows, 57 percent of respondents said the programs "show some truth but are mostly distorted," and 25 percent said "they are totally made up."[12] These days, viewers expect that every aspect of TV is manufactured. Even the jokes on late-night television that seem to be ad-libbed are carefully scripted. "Yet we accept it all without blinking," Stark writes.[13]

A media critic might be concerned about this zombie-like attitude on the part of media consumers. Fans of reality TV need to think twice about a medium that claims to represent a "reality" manipulated and edited to heighten drama to impossible proportions. Reality TV is not real. And it's rarely honest about its dishonesty.

Is Reality Television Independent?

As already noted, reality TV, by its nature, is cheap content. Scripts do not need to be written. Most of the "talent," recruited from the ranks of people desperate to validate their existence by appearing on the screen, is unpaid. This formula equates to giant profits for large media corporations like News Corporation, which owns Fox, home to *American Idol*. Add in funds from co-sponsors—advertisers who plug their products on reality TV shows—and listen for a hefty "cha-ching" as the cash piles up.

What might independent content look like? It would be free from the biases that come from corporate ownership and from its advertising sponsors. The content would not concern itself with making its sources (contestants) look good or bad. The content would not pander to its audience or to socially acceptable ideologies. Even an open-minded critic concludes that independent content is a rare commodity. Most media land on a continuum from mild bias to complete sell-out.

On the most independent end of the spectrum lie documentary-style shows such as *An American Family*. Because public broadcast funds don't come directly from advertisers, the show seemed free of commercial bias. Family members were not given a major cola brand to drink on camera or notable car to drive because of paid product placement. The complications that arose in family life—marital strife and a gay son coming out to his parents—during the year of filming were not glossed over to comfort a 1970s audience. This was not the impossibly happy family fodder offered up by 1950s sit-coms like *Leave It to Beaver*. As reality television goes, *An American Family* was on the independent end of the spectrum.

On the opposite end of the independence spectrum are contrived shows that operate as one-hour advertisements interspersed with commercial breaks. Product placement and brand integration are telltale signs that content is contrived to deliver audience eyeballs to advertisers. In the Fox network talent show *The X Factor*, contestants perform on a stage adorned with a Pepsi logo. Judges drink from Pepsi cups, and the soft drink is mentioned numerous times. No surprise, then, that the show's sponsor is not Coca-Cola.

Product placement as a form of advertising has been around since the 1890s when French filmmakers Auguste and Louis Lumiere promoted a soap company in a silent film. Today, product placement in reality television programs outpaces that in scripted television shows. A Nielsen compilation ranked product placement occurrences and number of episodes in 2011.[14] Of the 10 programs with the most product placement in 2011, 9 were reality shows. No. 6 on the product placement list was *Extreme Makeover: Home Edition*, a show that remodels the homes of needy families. The make-over crew shops at Sears for Pella Windows and Kenmore appliances, making regular mention of the store and brands. Tyson donates 10,000 pounds of chicken to one community and shots ensue of the truck with a Tyson logo. In 31 episodes, *Extreme Makeover* chalked up 224 product placements.

Who's No. 1? One of the most-watched show turns out to boast the most product placements, as well. In the 39 episodes of *American Idol* that ran in 2011, products and brands were notably featured 577 times. "Judges sip from large cups emblazoned with Coca-Cola logos, viewers are encouraged to text/call from their AT&T wireless phones, and Ford showcases weekly 'music videos' that feature contestants driving their vehicles," write Jill Weinberger and Joseph O'Dell at CNBC.[15] Sponsors pay around $50 million a year for placement in the show.

Although some reality TV might accurately and independently capture real human experiences, most contemporary reality TV cleverly packages fake drama to deliver audiences to advertisers. That's not independent.

Is Reality Television Productive?

In an episode of *Jersey Shore*, Nicole "Snooki" Polizzi drinks, dances, and accidentally urinates on the floor at a club. She heads to the bathroom to rinse off and spray herself with perfume. She calls this a "shore" shower. Later in the episode, she diagnoses herself with a urinary tract infection that she decides to treat with tequila. "Drinking when you have UTI is kind of like a pain killer," she advises.

Snooki's character had a simple approach to life that includes "gym, tan, laundry." When her roommate Mike annoyed her, she cussed and threw food at him. She was stylish in her own way, wore plenty of makeup, and drank excessive amounts of alcohol occasionally. Audiences laughed at Snooki and her roommates. They were entertaining. But did Snooki's real-life "guidette"[16] character provide a productive model for millions of viewers who watched this top-rated cable series?

As noted previously, media effects are constantly occurring whether we notice them or not. In his *Media Literacy* textbook, W. James Potter classifies effects into two categories: manifest effects and process effects.[17] Manifest effects include results we can see or hear. If a teacher catches herself saying "It's on like Donkey Kong" to students, it might be because the teacher is emulating Snooki, who says that in old episodes of *Jersey Shore*.

Process effects are the influences that media messages have on our ideas about ourselves, our relationships, and our behaviors. Over time, media messages shift our perspectives on acceptable attitudes and actions. We begin to see the world differently after repeated exposures to messages that might challenge our personal values. If we frequently see characters using violence to solve problems on TV, we may not manifest the behavior right away or ever. That depends on where our values baseline started out. The person raised by pacifist parents has a baseline lower than the person raised, say, in an aggressive household. But both parties, after enough time and exposure to media messages, could be expected to shift their perspectives on violence as a reasonable means to solve a problem. Process effects are the precursors of manifest effects. We think it; then we do it. That's what gives media narratives like those told through reality TV the potential to be productive—or not.

Media content exerts more influence on people with less knowledge of the world. An individual living far from New York or New Jersey has no knowledge of what a guido or guidette's life in New Jersey is like. That person has no basis of comparison for Snooki and her roommates. The more that person watches, the more Snooki might seem to be an authentic cultural expression. "As you increase your amount of viewing," Potter writes, "you are more likely to believe the real world is like the TV world."[18]

A few reality TV shows might boast altruistic motives— a cosmetic make-over for a distressed woman or a newly remodeled home for a needy family. That's a productive social value. And, it's fun to watch an unknown talent get discovered on a reality performance show, even if the circumstances are less-than-real. Overall, though, it'd be difficult to make a case that these shows influence human audiences to become better ancestors. Reality TV makes no attempt to hide its modus operandi, its appeal to our inner animals, the self-absorbed primates of our pre-evolutionary history. Think of reality TV as cheesy puffs in your mental environment. If we're going to watch 'em—consume responsibly.

BE THE CRITIC

Decide the value of reality TV shows that you or your friends might watch.

- Watch three episodes of a reality TV show carefully, taking detailed notes. Keep an open mind. You are a critic, not a cynic.

- Observe what scenes are included. Imagine what scenes are being left out. Does the content honestly depict "reality"?

- Count the times you see products featured in the shows. This includes brands of beverages, clothing, vehicles, toys, or other media content. Is the show independent of advertising influence?

- Try to discern what messages might emerge from the content. Are these messages productive? Might they prompt audiences to become "better ancestors"?

- Give the show a rating between 1 (not so hot) and 10 (great) based on your observations and the answers to the above questions.

SATIATE YOUR CURIOSITY

- You can find episodes of *Candid Microphone* on You-Tube or other websites that archive historic radio shows.

- CNBC created an informative slideshow based on the prime-time TV shows with the most product placement. It's at the CNBC website. http://www.cnbc.com/id/45884892/Primetime_Shows_With_the_Most_Product_Placement?slide=1

- *Quiz Show*, a 1994 film directed by Robert Redford, fictionalizes the infamous 1950s television scandals. Watch it.

Video Games

"A game was actually the first entertainment medium that made me cry. So I thought at the time, if I could make a game that [would] also not just move people to tears but make them feel like a better person after they play, that would be awesome."

—Designer Jenova Chen[1]

Millions of people are playing basketball about now, reliving famous games as legendary athletes like Michael Jordan and Larry Bird. Millions are answering the "Call of Duty" and arming themselves against enemy forces. Plenty more are fighting zombies or farming virtual acreage via their social networking site. Tens of thousands have assumed the role of Commander Shepard (male or female, race optional) to fight an epic battle for the survival of Planet Earth in the "Mass Effect" video game trilogy.

To those not enmeshed in the video-gaming world, players appear to be merely sitting in front of a screen, pushing controls on a keyboard or handheld device and sometimes talking out loud to, well, nobody in the room. To the player, however, the game opens up a world of experience, challenge, excitement—and even new friendships with other online game players.

The public's appetite for popular video games shows no signs of diminishing. A basketball game sequel "NBA 2K14" shipped 5 million copies in its first few months of sales. Around 3.5 million copies of "Mass Effect 3" were shipped in first week of sales. More than 50 million copies of various "Call of Duty" iterations have been sold.[2] The popular Facebook game "Farmville" has been installed more than 100 million times, and more than 8 million people played the game daily in 2013, according to a social media analytics firm.[3] "Candy Crush Saga" was the most downloaded iPhone app of 2013, with 500 million downloads.[4]

Games are profitable, rivaling many blockbuster movies. "Call of Duty: Modern Warfare 2" broke records with its release in 2009. The game, created for $40–50 million, achieved at least $1 billion in sales. The video game industry has global reach, with total revenue of $65 billion in 2011, reported Reuters.[5] Game fans are loyal, waiting in line to buy new spin-offs at midnight on a given release date. Fans become entrenched in relationships forged through online role-playing games like "World of Warcraft."

As video games are fast becoming one of mass media's juiciest sources of revenue, game companies invest more in developing new hits. Game development teams spend millions conceiving, writing, developing graphics, programming, hiring voice actors, and composing soundtracks for video games. They spend millions marketing the game. By one account, a marketing team spent twice as much to advertise and market a recent "Call of Duty" release than the company spent to create the game.[6]

Some observers worry about the addictive qualities of games, fearing that users spend too much time in front of screens—to the detriment of school or work or relationships. Psychologists who've studied video game effects point to links between violent video games and increased aggression.[7] Defenders of games refer to fears about video games as "hyperbolic" and "sensational."[8] In his book, *Videogames*, James Newman writes that social critics are suspicious and distrustful of rising interest in video games. This happens with the introduction of any new medium into society. In the early days of motion pictures, social critics feared that movies would corrupt young people. Rock music in the 1950s was feared as the precursor of social breakdown. Comic books could only mean cultural chaos was imminent. Newman suggests that these types of fears are blown out of proportion by those who suspect popular media of harmful effects without fully investigating these media forms.[9] A media critic, as we've seen, looks carefully at a medium before judging its impact, detrimental or otherwise, on the world citizenry.

Origins of Video Games

Defining video games and examining their origins and evolution begin the media critic's journey. A video game is entertainment on some type of computer, from phones to consoles to laptop PCs. You can play by yourself or with others through a networked environment.[10] If you haul the Jenga game out of the closet for family game night, you can play with everyone in the room. If you load the Jenga app onto your iPhone, you can play with people in your house, students from your school, your cousin in Atlanta, Georgia, or a stranger in Melbourne, Australia.

Considered the first video game, a simple game called "Tennis for Two." It was created in 1958 by nuclear physicist William Higinbotham so that folks would have some fun with a computer while visiting the Brookhaven National Laboratory. The game brought interest to the otherwise not-terribly-exciting research on early computers, computers so huge that they filled an entire room. People lined up to play the game, which featured glowing moving dots on a small screen.

In 1961, computer programmer Steve Russell at MIT wrote an interactive game—"Space Wars." The game caught on at institutions that had computers, including Stanford and the University of Utah. A Utah engineering student, Nolan Bushnell, who worked at a local arcade to pay his way through school, played "Space Wars" and came up with a brilliant idea. After he graduated, he hunkered down in his garage and, in 1971, created the first coin-operated video game based on "Space Wars." Although his invention was a flop, Bushnell found two friends willing to invest $250 each in his new video game company—Atari.

In 1972, Atari released "Pong." Before long, arcade games like "Space Invaders," "Pac-Man," "Ms. PacMan," and "Donkey Kong" were to be found everywhere. With the release of the cartridge-based console Atari 2600, the arcade games loved by many could be played at home. Oh, the quarters that were saved!

While Atari released simple action games for the public in arcades and later through its home system, a more complex narrative gaming trend was beginning to take hold in the academic realm. Cave enthusiast and computer programmer Will Crowther created a text-based adventure game: "Colossal Cave Adventure."

Crowther, a divorced father of two, wanted a game that he could play with his daughters. His adventure involved exploring a cave, solving a puzzle, and encountering creatures like an ax-throwing dwarf. The language of the game became part of the culture. Frustrated cave explorers might find themselves lost in the cave—as the game repeated: "You are in a maze of twisty passages, all alike." The line was adopted by computer hackers and programmers and still serves as a kind of inside joke today.

The game also served as an early example of a compelling puzzle that sucked up the time and attention of gamers. "The game spread like wildfire across the Internet," writes historian Rick Adams about a 1981 adaptation of "Cave Adventure," "inspiring such obsessive efforts to solve the game that it is rumored numerous college seniors did not graduate that year as a result."[11]

In 1985, a Japanese playing card company that had invested heavily in video games released the Nintendo Entertainment System in the United States. A year later, Nintendo released the "Legend of Zelda," a game that would serve as a new model for programmers. In "Zelda," players could make more choices about where to move their character. The game environment offered many routes to winning and much to explore along the way. "Zelda" laid the groundwork for best-selling games like "Mass Effect." The first-person shooter genre kicked off with the release of "Doom" in 1993. "Doom" could be played with others over computer networks. "World of Warcraft" was right around the corner.

Nowadays, according to the Entertainment Software Association, about 114 million Americans play video games regularly. Only about 25 percent are under age 18. About half are 18–49 years old—and 26 percent are 50 or older. Not all video game players are guys, either. About 40 percent of video gamers are female.[12]

Chances are that most humans in industrialized nations like the United States will play a game or two—or give birth to a child who wants to play. Or end up with a partner who spends more time in front of a screen than talking to her or his mate. A cynic might quickly conclude that video games are giant wasters of time—or even that violent games will have negative effects on players. A media critic looks closely at games of all types, evaluating their role in our lives by asking whether games are honest, independent, and, especially applicable in the game of games, productive.

Are Video Games Honest?

Unlike journalism and reality television, most video games make no real claims at conveying "truth" or being honest depictions of lived experience. A game like "The Sims" may seem to approximate real life—as the cartoon-like environment includes an avatar representing the player. The avatar must get a job, find friends, self-educate, exercise, eat, and even use the bathroom regularly. The goal of the game might be to advance in a career or to better your living circumstances through acquiring friends or decorating a house and yard. It's realistic in some ways, perhaps, but in other ways the game represents a working version of a popular American myth: if you try hard, you can succeed. The game's architecture confers success in generous doses to the central character. And, if something goes awry—and your avatar dies in a house fire—you can simply restart the game. It's a life simulation of a rarified, very safe, very privileged existence in the Western world.

Similarly, the "Mass Effects" science fiction series has been lauded for how accurately key facets of the game represent reality. A *Scientific American* article notes that as game players fly a spaceship across the universe, they encounter star systems and planets that are "torn from the annals of the real exoplanets, gussied up a little but still recognizable."[13] Players can virtually experience the variety of planet types—gassy, rocky, watery, and composed of various elements. "It's a surprisingly good representation of what we now think is really out there," writes Caleb A. Scarf, director of Columbia University's multidisciplinary Astrobiology Center.[14]

In fact, the immersive qualities of video games have been tapped for their educational potential since the early days of video gaming. Remember "Colossal Cave Adventure," mentioned earlier as an example of a narrative text-based game? The cave in the game faithfully reproduced the Bedquilt Cave system in Kentucky, a system that connects to the better-known Mammoth Caves. The game's programmer, an early explorer of the cave system, used computer aids to create a map of the system. The cave game was so accurate that one experienced gamer and spelunker found her gaming experience came in handy when exploring the Bedquilt cave system for the first time.

Educational games—even journalistic ones—are increasing in popularity. At the website for the *U.S.S. Constitution* Museum in Boston, Massachusetts, visitors can play the role of a young sailor aboard the famous ship "Old Iron-sides" during the War of 1812. An interactive game at the *New York Times* offers readers this challenge: "You Fix the Budget." Players make choices about cuts to military spending or medical care for the poor in an attempt to balance the federal budget. The game helps users see the complexities that underlie decisions about federal spending and taxation.

Even more popular video games, created to be profitable more than educational, may offer truthful insights about an event in the news. The setting of "Infamous 2" is a New Orleans experiencing the aftermath of Hurricane Katrina. The details of the game's Flood Town closely resemble New Orlean's 9th Ward, which experienced devastating flooding after the 2005 hurricane. The video game portrays the area as "a flooded ruin of clapboard houses and soaked stores. People wander through it. Living room furniture rests on roofs above a tide that has covered roads and spilled through doorways. Some roofs are spray-painted with pleas for help. One roof bears the telltale markings that were painted on the sides of homes during the post-Katrina search for survivors and dead bodies," describes one reviewer. "*Infamous 2* is an argument that games can perform a valuable service. They can be virtual tragedy simulators."[15]

Most games make no claims about honesty. Fantasy characters in make-believe situations might live or die—but video game life always includes a restart option. A few games, however, can operate as educators about geography, science—and even events in the news.

Are Video Games Independent?

What factors influence the making of video games? Audience demand might top the list. Also, video games might be crafted as tools for advertising or public relations, as is the case for games designed around children's breakfast cereals or a game developed by the U.S. military for recruitment. Like other media, the question of independence in video games may vary on a case-by-case basis.

Many game developers study what audiences want and attempt to give this to them. If gory, realistic violence seems to be selling, the gaming industry develops games that are more violent, more gory, more realistic. In "Sniper Elite," a World War II shooter released in 2005, players can watch their bullets enter a human target in slow motion. In "Sniper Elite 2," the sequel, as bullets enter—still in slow motion—the victim's clothing and skin pull back to reveal a skeleton and organs that explode in a dramatic, slow-motion burst of blood.[16] For a while, gore might have created buzz about a game. By the end of the first decade of the twenty-first century, however, carefully rendered details like exploding organs seemed standard fare. The game designer who leaves these out might not sell as many games.

Like other media, the influence of video games has been tapped by the persuasion industries—public relations and advertising. This trend affects independence as well. In the first decade or so of the twenty-first century, product placement in video games was all the rage. Advertisements appeared within video games. Skateboarders use Nokia cell phones within the game play of a Tony Hawk video game or SonyEricsson phones playing "Tom Clancy's Splinter Cell." In one version of "Guitar Hero," a player sees advertisements for KFC. Media effects researchers note that when specific product advertisements were placed within games, fondness for those products increased among game players.

Before long, though, large companies did not need to insert their products into games. Instead, the companies hired game designers and put their own interactive games online. At Nesquik.com, a young person can learn about healthful activities in the great outdoors. But he can also play a handful of games—surfing the Nesquik® bunny in a Mario-style game that involves catching beach balls and avoiding sharks or thunderclouds or unscrambling letters to make a word. A Pop-Tart® website features a memory game that involves matching various Pop-Tart flavors that include chocolate fudge, chocolate chip, hot fudge sundae, and Limited Edition Marshmallow Hot Chocolate. Tasty, right?

A game's independence might also be affected by the goals of game creators. The U.S. Army crafted an unabashed promotional video game: "America's Army." Produced for about $33 million, as of 2009, the game has extended to several sequels. "American Army" bills itself as "one of the ten most popular PC action games played online." The game's website includes links to community forums that have sprouted up around the game, its social media pages on Facebook and Twitter, an "America's Army" comic series, and free "America's Army" downloads like screensavers. The game offers players all over the world "the most authentic military experience available, from exploring the development of soldiers in individual and collective training to their deployment in simulated missions."[17]

The U.S. Army makes no secret about use of the game as a recruitment tool—and it appears to be working.[18] But a report from the American Civil Liberties Union finds fault with the "U.S. military's recruiting tactics that target children as young as 11 and disproportionately target low-income youth and students of color."[19] The game has also been criticized for its unrealistic depictions of death. In a version of the game designed for young players, a player who is shot simply sits down. When questioned by a journalist about the game's mellow depiction of fatalities, game project deputy director Chris Chambers replied, "We want to reach young people to show them what the Army does . . . We can't reach them if we are over the top with violence and other aspects of war that might not be appropriate."[20]

"America's Army" demonstrates the potential that exists for a well-produced game to become a powerful tool in the hands of a public opinion shaper. The independence of video games can be compromised by a game company's for-profit agenda—or by a need to promote Pop-Tarts or the U.S. Army.

Are Video Games Productive?

Video games waste our time, challenge our brains, increase our hand-eye coordination, cause us to procrastinate on homework, invade our dreams, and teach us. Are they productive? Sure. Does that mean productive in ways that make us better ancestors? Again, this varies on a case-by-case basis. A media critic studies not only the game to answer this question—but also the gamer and how he or she handles the potentially addictive media substance.

Let's start with some positive reports. Video games might offer potential as useful educational tools. Supporters of so-called serious games contend that games could provide appropriate—even better—educational tools for young people raised in an interconnected environment with Facebook, PlayStations, and smartphones. A University of Southern California (USC) study lists examples, including:

- Massachusetts Institute of Technology's Games to Teach project, which works on games for math, science, and engineering education.

- SuperNintendo's games designed for children dealing with health issues: Bronkie the Brachiosaurus (asthma); Packy & Marlon (diabetes); and Rex Ronin (smoking prevention).

- United Nations Food Force, a downloadable game about the fight against world hunger.

- Kellogg Creek Software's Power Politics, a U.S. presidential election campaign simulator.

The USC researchers recruited 100 college students to learn about physiology—some using "Metalloman," a game designed for undergraduates, and others reading text and reviewing graphics similar to a textbook. The students playing the game performed better than the textbook readers on a test about the material. The researchers suggest that the enjoyment of entertainment motivates players to gain new knowledge. "All forms of play are learning and all forms of learning are play," the researchers propose. "The separation of learning and play is artificially imposed" in some educational environments.[21]

Games can be productive. But video games can also be addictive. That could mean trouble for a student's grades or an adult's chances at work success. Gaming "addicts" can become so involved in a game that they forget to go to work or school—or even to eat, drink, and sleep. In extreme (and rare) instances, addiction can be fatal. In 2012, an 18-year-old died after a 40-hour session playing the popular video game "Diablo 3" at an Internet café in Taiwan.[22] Turns out that sitting or being sedentary for long periods can lead to health problems—including deadly blood clots.

More causes for concern come from what psychiatrists have found to be the effects of violence in video games. In an article in *Psychology Today*, Darcia Narvaez argued that violent games also have several negative effects. First, the pretend violence is rewarded in games—bringing pleasure to the player. Second, the violent behavior is practiced over and over and over, with rewards increasing in frequency as the player's skills at violence are honed. Finally, the games "can harm the final stages of brain development in young adults, leaving them with a less than mature decision-making system and diminished empathy for others."[23]

Do Narvaez's findings apply to "Candy Crush Saga," a simple game that delights and puzzles millions? Probably not. But what about "Angry Birds," the goal of which is to catapult avians at clumsily housed pigs, destroying the structures and the pigs that reside helplessly within? Identifying the violence in media might seem arbitrary to some and restricting the medium might be criticized as a violation of the First Amendment's free-speech guarantees. The latter view was expressed by a Supreme Court justice in the majority decision to not allow states to restrict video game sales to minors.

In June 2011, the U.S. Supreme Court ruled against a California law that banned selling violent games to kids. The entertainment industry had lobbied heavily against the law—and so did some free-speech advocates. Banning sales of games violated the First Amendment's prohibition on government's censoring or limiting media content agreed a majority of the Supreme Court justices. "Like books, plays and movies, video games communicate ideas," wrote Justice Antonin Scalia. "No tradition in this country [allows] specially restricting children's access to depictions of violence. . . . Grimms' *Fairy Tales*, for example, are grim indeed."[24]

Where does this leave us, overall, with the question of productivity for video games? Games are powerful learning tools, it seems. But who's doing the teaching? The best-selling games, those that users spend hours, days, or months playing, aren't teaching geography or math. Some are persuasive tools for groups with an agenda—such as the U.S. Army. Popular immersive games may contribute to increased aggression as psychologists have noted. Game addiction has physical and social consequences that aren't positive for the players. For now, while games have the potential to be used to make humans better ancestors, this potential is largely untapped. Proceed with awareness.

BE THE CRITIC

- Think of two games you've enjoyed—one video game and one physical game in which play happens without a computer.

- Relive the experience of playing these games, preferably with a friend or partner.

- Describe the games in depth. What kind of play occurs in the game? What's easy—or hard or challenging? Does the game have a winner or loser? Is anything learned by this game? Take some notes.

- Analyze the two games, looking for meaningful patterns—similarities and contrasts between the two experiences. Interpret what these patterns might mean.

- Evaluate your experience. Does one gaming mode seem "better" than another? More engaging and fun? More educational? Write a few sentences about your conclusions.

- Share your conclusions via social networks, telling classmates or parents, or by making poster or YouTube video.

SATIATE YOUR CURIOSITY

- Play the World Food Programme's "Free Rice" game. Designed for English-language learners, the game offers positive reinforcement for correct answers by donating 10 grains of rice per question to end hunger in developing nations. http://freerice.com

- Play an interactive federal budget game at the *New York Times*. http://www.nytimes.com/interactive/2010/11/13/weekinreview/deficits-graphic.html

- Find Dr. Craig Anderson's list of 11 myths and facts about the effects of violent video games. http://www.apa.org/science/about/psa/2003/10/anderson.aspx

- Play the first interactive text game "Colossal Cave Adventure." http://jerz.setonhill.edu/if/gallery/adventure/index.html

- Watch PBS Frontline's "Growing Up Online," http://www.pbs.org/wgbh/pages/frontline/kidsonline/ and "Digital Nation," http://www.pbs.org/wgbh/pages/frontline/digitalnation/

9 Recorded Music and Celebrity Musicians

"Songs remain. They last. The right song can turn an emperor into a laughing stock, can bring down dynasties. A song can last long after the events and the people in it are dust and dreams and gone. That's the power of songs."

—Neil Gaiman, *Anansi Boys*[1]

Music entertains us, gets our feet tapping on the floor. Songs inspire wild dancing, hands over our heads, not caring what anyone thinks. Words and melodies sooth us, lull, and provoke. Music can arguably shape culture, as well. In 1963, Joan Baez recorded "We Shall Overcome," an anthem for the civil rights movement that remains a hopeful theme song for activists of all kinds today. In 1983, U2 captured the world's attention with its recording of "Sunday Bloody Sunday," raising awareness of political strife in Ireland. The music video for "Same Love," recorded by Macklemore and Ryan Lewis, won a 2013 Video Music Award for Best Video with a Social Message. The song was dubbed an "equality anthem" by MTV, and the musicians were introduced at VMA awards ceremony by openly gay NBA basketball star Jason Collins and the Harlem rapper A$AP Rocky.

Music provides audiences with new ways of looking at important topics and with heightened levels of awareness. Recording artist Michael Franti says: "We can't change foreign policy or fix global warming, but music has the power to provide a different perspective of how people view the world."[2] Franti, whose own music is infused with optimism about social activism, says a range of music, from hip-hop to funk, influenced his adolescence. "It really shaped my consciousness and it made me think beyond my immediate borders and so I went into it believing that music is a way to express one's self," he says.[3]

Artistic expression through tunes and lyrics is as much about the musician as it is about the recorded song. Like actors and athletes, musical artists can become media celebrities, and the narratives in news media and gossip publications wield almost as much power as the songs they perform. The concept of "stardom" for musicians evolved hand in hand with music recording technology. Before the 1800s, music was performed live in living rooms, churches, town squares, and concert halls. When recording technology was developed and multiple copies of one sound recording could be made, people could access music in new ways. A meaningful song could be played again and again as a record on a phonograph. The record label included the name of the performers, some of whom attracted more listeners than others. From this practice, the celebrity musician emerged. Recording artists were touted as personalities that inspired strong emotions among fans.

Young people lined up to see Frank Sinatra or swooned at the sound of Elvis Presley's voice in the late 1950s. In the 1960s, the Beatles captured the attention of the world, with song lyrics that often challenged a social status quo and attracted frenzied throngs of teens. In 1982, Michael Jackson released *Thriller*, the best-selling album in music history as of this writing and winner of eight Grammy awards. Nirvana's Kurt Cobain rose to international fame in the 1990s with the album *Nevermind*, an album that channeled the angst of so-called Generation X.

Although the advent of the Internet shifted the music industry, the potential for recording artists to reach millions with their music has never been greater. In the first decade of the twenty-first century, Beyonce received 64 gold (sales of 500,000) and platinum (sales of a million units) certifications for albums, digital songs, ringtones, and music videos, according to record industry reports.[4] Beyonce and hip-hop artist Jay-Z have both used their celebrity to draw attention to political issues, including opposition to Florida's Stand Your Ground laws, which they related to the shooting of Trayvon Martin, an unarmed 17-year-old, in 2012.

Aware of the medium's power, the music media critic buckles down and listens up. As art, recorded music should be examined for honesty in the content of songs and the mass media narrative told about lives of celebrity musicians. Recorded music should be examined for its independence from artistic control or censorship by major record labels, audiences, advertisers, or activist groups. Finally, a critic evaluates the productive potential of music and the images of celebrity musicians as positive cultural forces that move audiences in the direction of becoming better ancestors. That said, the terrain of recorded music, like many other popular media, is complicated. Let's dig right in.

Is Recorded Music Honest?

An examination of recorded music's honesty involves looking at the content of songs—and at the celebrity musician's image as cultivated in mass media. As with other media, this critique needs to be done on a case-by-case basis.

Let's start with Miley Cyrus, once better known for her starring role in the Disney Channel's *Hannah Montana* TV series, who recorded a cute, catchy tune "Party in the U.S.A." in 2009. The lyrics relate the story of an awkward girl in a cardigan finding herself in Hollywood for the first time and awed by stardom and stilettos. But, when she hears her favorite songs on the radio, she knows she's going to be OK. Certified six times platinum by the Recording Industry Association of America, the song was loved by young people and tolerated as harmless by their parents.

Honest lyrics? The song depicts the story of a naïve innocent landing in Los Angeles and feeling insecure. Far from naïve or innocent, Cyrus, daughter of a recording star and seasoned TV star, was singing a story not likely to have emerged from her own experience. Nonetheless, adolescents might relate to this character's uncertainty and remedy all by belting out the song's refrain.

Similarly, in the first few years of his career, Justin Bieber's music, overall, remained in wholesome territory. His 2010 song "Baby" is a simple song of love and devotion with a catchy innocuous refrain. In the popular song "Boyfriend," lyrics promise an enduring relationship, the behavior of a "gentleman," and manage to reference Buzz Lightyear, the toy astronaut from *Toy Story*. Bieber's image, cultivated in mass media narratives, was of a clean-cut heartthrob, a remarkable young man of whom parents would approve.

No sex, no drugs, no controversial politics.[5] Honest? Nothing to suggest otherwise.

Writes business analyst Ira Kalb of the early days of Cyrus and Bieber: "Parents saw them as great role models for their kids since they both looked squeaky clean and appeared to espouse the family values so many parents want their kids to follow."[6] And then the fans grew up. And so did the celebrity musicians.

Cyrus posed topless for the cover of *Rolling Stone* in 2013, twerked[7] at televised music awards, and performed provocatively in her wildly popular music video "Wrecking Ball." The result was loads of media coverage—complete with clueless adults googling the word *twerk*. Cyrus's YouTube video for "Wrecking Ball" nabbed 300 million hits in its first two months online.[8] Bieber transformed into a tattooed bad boy with an arrest record, reports of encounters with Brazilian prostitutes, and an edgy Instagram account with 15.6 million followers. Are these honest depictions of the stars' passages into adulthood?

Analyst Kalb attributes the shifts to a deliberate rebranding strategy. "Their behavior," he writes, "is part of a deliberate marketing plan to shatter their goody-two-shoes images and create new ones that fit the desires of their changing audiences. . . . If you judge them by the numbers—followers on social media, brisk record sales, and sold-out tours, their rebranding plans are working really well."[9] Cyrus and Bieber, it seems, are carefully shaped products designed for mass appeal. TV commercials are more honest than the music of these stars—because at least we know that TV commercials are trying to sell us something.

In contrast to the slick marketing of some popular music are songs and celebrity musicians who put their careers on the line to be forthright with their audiences. One memorable example, the Grammy Award–winning music of the Dixie Chicks was banned at country music stations in 2003 after lead singer Natalie Maines told a London audience that she was "ashamed" that U.S. president George W. Bush was from Texas.[10] Maines's comments came just as the United States began the Iraq War and were considered unpatriotic by some. Others viewed her words as an honest expression of her thoughts on the war.

Many artists used their music and lyrics to express their opinions about the wars in Iraq and Afghanistan in first decade of the 2000s. Songwriter Tom Waits channeled the thoughts of a soldier in the ballad, "Day After Tomorrow," in considering the perspective of the so-called enemy soldier who also prays to God in hopes of not dying in war.[11] Waits performed the song on *The Daily Show with Jon Stewart*, with Stewart referring to the song as his own "Moment of Zen."

Eminem recorded the song "Mosh" in 2004 and released it during George W. Bush's campaign for reelection. The song suggests that political leaders aren't listening to their constituents and advises immediate action.[12] Taking a side in a political showdown is a risky career move. Some loathed Eminem for it. Others loved the song. Democratic blogger Markos Moulitsas called the song's music video "hopeful and disturbing and honest" at *The Daily Kos*. "Watching this video is one of those experiences that just *changes* you," Moulitsas wrote. "*Mosh* is political art that, at the same time, speaks in an authentic and specific voice."[13]

Music can be honest and recording artists have the ability to express something real in a deep and meaningful way. But honest art can be uncomfortable. Music that challenges popular opinion or that seems controversial might not attract as large an audience as the palatable drug-free love songs of a teen heartthrob. The recording artist who seeks to be honest faces resistance from a for-profit industry and marketers who know what music "sells" both within the industry and to a large swath of fans.

Is Recorded Music Independent?

The role of popular music in contemporary times is a complex one. Making art can become conflated with fame and making money. The desire for fame and for money may challenge the independence of the art itself.

The legendary music of Bob Dylan seemed to many to be an example of truly independent artistic expression. Dylan's lyrical advice includes the line: "To live outside the law you must be honest."[14] And yet, it seemed Dylan's independence came under fire when he sold the rights to "The Times They Are A'Changing" to a Canadian bank. In 2004, Dylan appeared in a series of advertisements for Victoria's Secret. Fans wondered if Dylan had "sold out." One critic noted that Dylan might be playing a practical joke on the world. *Slate's* Seth Stevenson cites newspaper reports of a 1965 interview in which Dylan says, jokingly, that one thing might "tempt him to sell out . . . 'ladies undergarments.'"[15] At least he was straightforward about it, right?

Money influences the honest reputation of a recording artist like Bob Dylan because it signals his willingness to suspend his independence and shill for a bank or a business like Victoria's Secret. Commercialism in music runs rampant today, as record companies license legendary music to commercial advertisers. Beatles' music has been used in ads for Target, Allstate Insurance, and Nike. Beatles drummer Ringo Starr appeared in a Pizza Hut ad—with another 1960s group, The Monkees. You say you want a revolution? Apparently eating corporate pizza crust-first qualifies.

Large record companies, subsidiaries of even larger media conglomerates, can exert some control over artists' creative process, watering down what might otherwise be robustly independent music. The experiences of popular 1990s grunge band Nirvana provide an interesting look at recording artists who wanted to make a statement—about the record industry of which they were a part.

At the height of Nirvana's popularity in the early 1990s, the band was booked to play for MTV's Video Music Awards. The band was enjoying fame after the issue of *Nevermind,* its first album released on a major record label. MTV executives expected Nirvana to play the band's most famous hit, "Smells Like Teen Spirit." But, instead, frontman Kurt Cobain wanted to play a new song, "Rape Me," that he'd written to channel feelings of artistic exploitation. The song was an "allegory of society's abuses" and a "personal metaphor for how he felt treated by the media, his managers, his bandmates, his addiction, and MTV," writes Charles R. Cross in a biography of Cobain.[16] MTV forbade Nirvana from performing the song, threatening to cancel Nirvana's performance and to not play the group's music videos on MTV. Cobain was unbending. MTV flexed its muscle with the band's managers, Gold Mountain, saying it would not play any of the other artists managed by Gold Mountain. It was a classic example of a corporate entity using its power for censorship of an uncomfortable message.

In the end, band members hit on a prank that seemed rebellious but didn't cost any jobs. Nirvana took the MTV stage, played the first few chords of the forbidden song. Cobain sang, "Rape me . . . Rape me," but within seconds, stopped as MTV execs ran to intervene. Bass player Krist Novoselic gave a feisty salute as the band launched quickly into "Lithium." Cobain sang, "I'm so happy cuz today I found my friends."[17]

Independent artistic expression might also be compromised during the distribution of music. For example, in 1993, Walmart stores would not sell Nirvana's album *In Utero,* which contained the song "Rape Me" and cover art that showed a human fetus. The store agreed to stock a revised version of the album the next year, however. The fetus art was changed to decorative flowers and the controversial song title "Rape Me" was edited so that Cobain was singing "Waif Me."[18]

To retain independence from the influence of large record companies, some artists record on or even start small independent record labels. Songwriter and guitarist Ani DiFranco formed an independent record label Righteous Records (now Righteous Babe Records) at age 19 to ensure that she wouldn't be snarled up in the kind of profit motives that would result in a compromise of her independence. Grammy-winning DiFranco writes songs about corporate greed, about loving a country that disappoints her, and about society's expectations of women.

In "I Am Not a Pretty Girl," she sings, wryly, about crafting a self-identity that's powerful and self-reliant. The Righteous Babe Foundation has championed causes from abortion rights to support for Hurricane Katrina victims. The National Organization of Women gave DiFranco the Woman of Courage Award in 2006.[19] "The world needs more radicals like Ani DiFranco: wry, sexy, as committed to beauty and joy as revolution," writes Will Hermes in *Rolling Stone*.[20]

In recent years, various music file-sharing tools have allowed new and emerging artists to promote their work—and, by some accounts, it's lessened the control of music companies over the artistic expression of recording artists. More independent artists are making more independent music, selling and sharing it online with no help from major record labels owned by large media corporations.

Although the commercial nature of music and the influence of corporate record labels may challenge the independence of recording artists and their music, many musicians have proven that they don't have to compromise their art.

Is Recorded Music Productive?

Some discussions about the effects of popular music might tend to focus on what's seen as its negative impact or bad influence, especially on young listeners. In 1990, the band Judas Priest was taken to court because parents and lawyers said the band's music had influenced the suicide attempts of two young men.[21] The band's accusers claimed that one song, if played backwards, encouraged the young men to "do it." The family's lawyers failed to prove that the band was linked to the suicides.

After a shooting rampage by two teenagers at Columbine High School in Colorado, shock-rock musician Marilyn Manson was fingered as a media influence. The teens may or may not have been fans of Manson's music. That didn't matter to critics who protested before Manson's concerts. In a *Rolling Stone* essay, however, Manson made a case for music—especially music that challenges an unhealthy status quo—as a positive influence in culture. "It is no wonder that kids are growing up more cynical; they have a lot of information in front of them," Manson writes. "Sometimes music, movies and books are the only things that let us feel like someone else feels like we do."[22]

If Manson is right, recorded music can be a productive social force that simply reassures listeners that others share our hopes, fears, and joys. John Lennon of The Beatles wrote a song famously advising us to "imagine all the people living life in peace." Did his song influence the entire world to give up its weapons of mass destruction? Nope. Did the lyrics affirm a segment of the audience who felt out of the norm for their peacenik-ness? Absolutely.

After September. 11, 2001, people living in the United States—and around the world—felt uncertain about the future. Everything seemed topsy-turvy to people living in what had seemed to be the permanently secure United States of America. Before the nation's vibe turned to one of patriotism and retribution, some creative thinking audio engineers remixed thoughtful rock songs into reflective tributes to the tragedy. In particular, U2's "Peace on Earth" and "Stuck in the Moment" were recrafted to include news audio clips from the day's events. The melding of the two forms—news media and U2's lead singer Bono singing a song recorded—and popular—before the tragedy seemed appropriate in the wake of the terrorist strike. The music soothed and united its audience, in contrast to the later political rhetoric that would divide the nation for the durations of long wars in Afghanistan and Iraq.

The Greek philosopher Plato, writing some 2,350 years ago, believed in music's intense influence—that music itself embodies physical and emotional states. The musician can transfer these states of being, whether good or bad, to the listeners. "Thus certain sorts of music would educate boys into living highly ethical lives while other sorts could educate them into baseness," writes music theorist Michael Linton of Plato's ideas.[23] Linton argues that music can be a productive force in some ways. It can help a human endure repetitive chores, encourage learning, and provide a means of self-reflection or illumination. But a song won't inject humanity with the universal will to act in a certain way. "Music is not a drug that incapacitates the listener and produces a predictable result," Linton writes. "A whole lifetime spent listening to Bach will not automatically make a woman love God. And—despite the warning of two generations of moralists—a lifetime listening to the Rolling Stones will not make a man fornicate."[24]

If a rock song doesn't instigate sexual activity—or provoke suicide or mass murder—then it stands to reason that it won't directly cause global social change. But it can certainly point us in the right direction and assure us that others feel as we do. Recorded music gives us a soundtrack to hum while we work to make the world better for our descendants.

BE THE CRITIC

- Check out *Billboard*'s charts to find out what songs, ringtones, and albums are the top-sellers. Watch the videos for the top 10 songs or so on YouTube. Take some notes, describing what you see in the video. What do these top artists look like? What kind of music do they play? What are the lyrics like?

- Track any patterns you observe in the popular music. What do the top hits have in common? How are they different?

- Consider what those patterns might mean. Is contemporary music more about what you look like? Do popular artists write thought-provoking lyrics?

- Make an in-depth evaluation of the top 10 songs you've observed. Are they honest, independent, and/ or productive?

- Write a letter to individual artists, record labels— or the folks at *Billboard*—telling them about your findings.

SATIATE YOUR CURIOSITY

- *BBC Magazine* asked readers to submit to its list of "20 Songs That Changed the World." http://www.bbc.com/news/magazine-21143345

- PBS *Frontline* documentary "The Way the Music Died" tracks a female solo recording artist and a new rock band comprised of former members of Guns & Roses and Stone Temple Pilots. Along the way, documentarians interview record industry insiders and music journalists about the state of the business.

- Explore independent record labels listed at the *NewPages Guide to Independent Record Labels*. http://www.newpages.com/npguides/music.htm

- Watch Nirvana's performance at the 1992 MTV Music Video Awards. http://www.youtube.com/watch?v=z8y5ibUBw1

10 Feature-length Documentaries

"It might make sense to ask what (or whom) a given documentary is for? Is it a goad to awareness, an incitement to action, a spur to further thought? A window? A mirror? The more you think about it, the less obvious the truth appears to be."

—A. O. Scott, film critic, *The New York Times*[1]

In 2003, global hamburger-mongering McDonald's had successfully quashed lawsuits claiming that Big Macs and chicken nuggets were health risks disguised as food. The court decisions inspired modern-day muckraker[2] Morgan Spurlock to make a documentary of himself eating nothing but McDonald's for a month. He'd work his way through everything on McDonald's menu—breakfast, lunch, and dinner. If a McDonald's employee made the offer, "Do you want to supersize that?" Spurlock would agree.

Spurlock gained 25 pounds that month. He also won a directing prize when his documentary movie, *Super Size Me,* was launched at the Sundance Film Festival in 2003. Some reviewers called his experiment an act of pseudo-science, a gimmick. Others thought the movie was funny and potentially life-changing. "The value of *Super Size Me* is not what happens during the movie, but what happens afterwards," writes reviewer C. A. Wolski. "In the great documentary tradition, the movie is really a jumping off point for audience members to discuss notions of diet, personal responsibility and 'corporate responsibility' (e.g., should a corporation be held liable for selling a product it admits isn't good for us)."[3]

When it comes to documenting reality in feature-length movies, the lines between information and entertainment blur, as *New York Times* film critic A. O. Scott suggests. The word *documentary* can describe nearly anything from *Blair Witch*–like cinéma vérité to a journalistic exploration of the state of news media like PBS *Frontline*'s "News Wars" to the *Jackass 3-D* experience. "Documentary is, at present, heterogeneous almost to the point of anarchy," Scott writes.[4] In this chapter, the word *documentary* is applied to feature-length movies that involve reporting and the telling of a nonfiction story.

Spurlock's month-long Big Mac munch, thought up in advance and performed for the camera, is an example of "stunt" journalism—where the reporter engages in an activity to be able to report his or her experiences. To some, it seemed a bit gimmicky or prefabricated to count as a serious exploration of the fast food industry.

But using a so-called gimmick in documentary movies, as Spurlock did, isn't unusual. For the movie *Bowling for Columbine*, a documentary that explores U.S. attitudes toward guns and gun control in the wake of the school shooting in Colorado, filmmaker Michael Moore drove a shooting victim to K-Mart corporate headquarters to confront company executives about K-Mart's ammunition sales. He filmed the encounter for his documentary.[5]

Broadcast news investigations have included stunt-like tactics. In 1992, ABC *PrimeTimeLive* reporters Lynne Dale and Susan Barnett investigated unsanitary meat-handling practices at a supermarket chain by getting jobs at the stores. They used cameras hidden in wigs and lipstick cases to record footage of expired meat being mixed with fresh beef for resale and barbecue sauce being dumped on aging chicken to mask its foul smell. Lawsuits ensued.[6]

Much documentary muckraking involves straightforward, in-depth reporting. In 1960, TV newsman Edward R. Murrow crafted the documentary, *Harvest of Shame*, depicting the dismal lives of migrant farmworkers in the United States. The award-winning documentary *An Inconvenient Truth* (2006), narrated by Al Gore, includes video footage of changing environments and interviews with scientists concerned about climate change, in addition to personal stories about Gore's own conversion to environmental activism. *An Inconvenient Truth* was directed by David Guggenheim, who went on to craft *Waiting for Superman*, a documentary that examines the inadequacies of public education in the United States. Guggenheim talks to parents, politicians, teachers, and activists, but his most important characters are the young people whose education depends on the chancy status of public schools.

As savvy media critics, we know how to examine stories in mass media messages like documentaries. We're familiar with the questions that need to be examined to decide whether a feature-length documentary is honest, independent, and productive.

Are Documentaries Honest?

An aware media consumer watches a feature-length news documentary knowing that the piece might have a bias. Spurlock, for example, didn't consume cheeseburgers, fries, and giant soft drinks for a month thinking his health would improve. And, when Guggenheim sets out in *An Inconvenient Truth* to turn Vice President Al Gore's climate change PowerPoint presentation into 100 minutes of dire warning about Earth's dismal future and sunken cities, we don't expect to be baffled by conflicting evidence. We do expect the case presented, however, to be accurate. If Spurlock says he gained 25 pounds, we'd like to believe he did. If Gore, who won the Nobel Peace Prize for his work on climate change, says polar bears are drowning because they can't swim far enough to make it to melting floes, well, we'd like to think he has some evidence for this. But, while most of the documentary's info was well-researched, the polar bear anecdote turned out to be a problem.

To back up, the award-winning documentary *An Inconvenient Truth* includes plenty of information other than threatened polar bears that passes fact-checking tests. The movie shows human impact on our environment with film of furiously flaming petroleum refineries and hideous plumes of filth rising from the smokestacks of manufacturing plants. That climate change is happening, that it caused by human activity, specifically increased greenhouse gasses created by industrial pollution, power plants, and our obsession with motor vehicles, is a view on which most scientists concur. But *Washington Post*'s Michael Dobbs chastised Gore for a few errant specifics,[7] including the assertion that polar bears are drowning because they couldn't swim the increasing distance between icebergs. They also might have died from storms or hypothermia, says Andrew Derocher, chair of the polar bear group at the World Conservation Union. Writes Dobbs: "In their zeal to draw attention to the cause, even Nobel Peace Prize laureates can make mistakes or shade the truth a little."[8]

A feature-length documentary is no small undertaking. It can take years of research, filming interviews, writing, editing video, and post-production to create 90 minutes of finished documentary. To commit to a project that time-consuming requires the kind of passion and urgency that comes from wanting to tell an untold story or to expose a neglected truth. Pursuing these goals while maintaining an even-handed approach is the key to honesty.

Are Documentaries Independent?

In 1989, Michael Moore made *Roger & Me*, in which he documents the effect of General Motors CEO Roger Smith's summary decision to close several auto plants in Flint, Michigan, despite GM's record profits. Moore funded his movie project by mortgaging his home and using money from a settlement in an unrelated lawsuit.[9] Being self-funded gave Moore independence. No media corporation paid the bills for *Roger & Me*, and so no profit-minded bosses could encourage formulaic content or discourage controversy. Moore's independence wasn't marred by commercialism, as Moore did not secure funding for strategically placing a can of cola in the hands of those he interviewed.

Corporate ownership and commercialism are two factors that influence the independence of most media, including documentary movies. First, let's look at corporate ownership and the profit motive of large media companies so we can see why independent documentaries might never get made. Many movies shown in U.S. cinemas are funded by large movie companies that are part of even larger media conglomerates. For example, the Walt Disney Co. makes movies through Walt Disney Pictures, Buena Vista, Touchstone Pictures, Pixar, Walt Disney Animation Studios, Marvel Studios, and Disneynature. If a giant media conglomerate like Disney is going to risk millions making a movie, the company's executives are going to exercise careful control over the movie's content.

What kinds of movies do major production companies want? Movies that sell—action films, comedies, romances. Movies that deviate too much from successful formulas might never get made. Unfortunately documentary movies are harder to fit into the formula.

Production companies have been willing to finance some documentaries, but these often face corporate challenges that threaten independence. Miramax Films financed Moore's 2004 documentary *Fahrenheit 9/11*, which critiques the motives of George W. Bush in going to war in Iraq after the terrorist attacks of September 11, 2001. At that time, Miramax was owned by the Walt Disney Company. News reports suggested that Disney hadn't known about its subsidiary's decision to fund the movie. The documentary's criticism of the Bush administration made the media company execs nervous. After all, it was an election year. Michael Moore's agent contended that Disney CEO Michael D. Eisner was worried that the company would be punished for releasing the film, possibly losing tax breaks Disney receives for its theme park, hotels, and other ventures in Florida—where George W. Bush's brother, Jeb Bush, was governor.[10] Unlike the independence Moore had in filming *Roger & Me*, it seemed that the *Fahrenheit 9/11* production's independence was threatened. Disney's Miramax dropped the movie.[11]

In the end, the independence of *Fahrenheit 9/11* was not compromised by the financing from a parent media corporation company. The project was saved by the willingness of an independent production company to take a chance on Moore. The risk paid off. But the larger lesson is that a movie's independence varies depending on who's paying the bills.

Because documentaries are expensive, funding them could be a risk to each movie's independence as it can be in the case of other forms of journalism and entertainment. Documentary makers like Moore and others who are interested in making real, informative, and entertaining movies have demonstrated that they'll go to some lengths to retain independence.

Are Documentaries Productive?

Can documentary movies make their viewers better ancestors—or at least contribute to positive change in society? Absolutely.

Even though Moore's *Fahrenheit 9/11* was a box office smash, Bush handily beat challenger John Kerry, a U.S. senator from Massachusetts, at the polls. But Moore's critical look at the Bush presidency, the war on terror, and the media response provoked debate on important issues. McDonald's announced its decision to dump the super-size option from its menu just a few months after the release of Spurlock's *Super Size Me*, although the company said the popularity of the movie had no impact whatsoever on its decision.

The first documentary to profoundly influence public opinion in the United States was broadcast journalist Edward R. Murrow's *Harvest of Shame*, which aired on CBS the day before Thanksgiving in 1960. Its goal was to increase awareness of the poor living conditions endured by migrant farmworkers—the people whose work made American feasts possible at Thanksgiving. Murrow interviewed workers who lived in squalid homes provided by growers and who worked for dismal wages.

Within a few years of Murrow's documentary, U.S. lawmakers had crafted the Farm Labor Contractor Registration Act of 1963. The new law didn't accomplish all of the changes that Murrow had outlined at the end of *Harvest of Shame*. But it did require worker crew leaders to be under a contract and licensed by the U.S. Department of Labor. By 1985, many more changes had been incorporated into a more wide-reaching federal law that required farmers to explain terms of employment—like wages and benefits—when a worker is hired. The housing provided for workers must meet local and federal housing standards. Vehicles used to transport workers must meet basic federal safety standards.[12]

Murrow's straightforward documentary is painfully honest. Although Murrow's report may seem biased in that it works to convince the audience that the life of the migrant farmworker is not to be envied, the documentary allows farmers and businessmen to make their cases for the workers' treatment. The documentary was productive in the best sense of the word—shaping public opinion and, eventually, the passage of relevant legislation.

A CBS report 50 years later lauded the influence of Murrow's documentary.[13] But the report also noted that the lives of migrant farmworkers are still plagued by numerous problems. Documentaries may raise awareness for a time. But audiences today might also quickly move on to the next hot topic. Perhaps, in the long run, the importance of Murrow's film lies not in creating awareness but in setting an example that others might follow. Many productive documentaries, such as *Roger & Me, Supersize Me,* and *An Inconvenient Truth,* would emerge in the coming decades.

These are merely a few examples of documentary films that help us better understand our role in contemporary existence.

BE THE CRITIC

- Pick a documentary to fact-check.

- Watch the documentary carefully several times, taking detailed notes. Identify the movie's central argument or claims.

- Identify the facts or evidence used to support those claims—from expert interviews to scientific studies or personal anecdotes.

- Using what you know about accessing reliable sources (see Appendix A), check out the facts. What do other experts say and do they differ? What scientific research supports the movie's claim? Does any verifiable information contradict the facts or evidence portrayed in the documentary?

- Evaluate the movie based on your findings. Is it a useful source of information or a biased propaganda piece—or a little of both?

- If you find facts that don't check out, write a letter or email to the filmmaker explaining your fact-checking work.

SATIATE YOUR CURIOSITY

- Check out the top documentaries (rated by profitability) since 1982 at Box Office Mojo. http://boxofficemojo.com/genres/chart/?id=documentary.htm

- Watch Morgan Spurlock's documentary *Pom Wonderful Presents the Greatest Movie Ever Sold* (2011). The movie documents Spurlock's attempts to finance a movie about product placement.

- Another good documentary to watch: *Happy* (2011) explores human happiness through interviews with happy people from all over the world—and psychological researchers who say they can measure happiness and figure out what makes people happy.

 **Animation**

"[Animation is] a liberating form that free associates like crazy and makes audiences see the world afresh."

—James Clarke[1]

In 1989, *The Simpsons* began airing on the Fox Network. The show was one of the first cartoons to run during the most sought-after airtime in the evenings. *The Simpsons* was a popular show about an average family of five, including beer-drinking, doughnut-eating Dad and his mischievous son Bart. At its start, parents and educators criticized the show for its unflattering portrayal of a U.S. family. In a speech to religious broadcasters, Pres. George H. W. Bush complained about *The Simpsons,* comparing the cartoon family unfavorably with *The Waltons*, a show about a Depression-era family who seemed to exemplify strong moral character. Said Bush in his speech: "We are going to try to strengthen American families so they're a lot more like *The Waltons* and a lot less like *The Simpsons.*" The crowd cheered wildly.

Not in the president's audience that day, perhaps, were those who felt *The Simpsons* represented a more authentic version of the American family in entertaining and useful ways. It was funny. It was real. After the president's speech, the cartoon family replied to the president in the next episode. The yellow-faced family is shown eating dinner in front of the TV set, watching actual footage of Bush on a cartoon TV. Smart-mouthed Bart offers a wry observation: "Hey, we're just like *The Waltons*, we're praying for an end to the Depression, too." This exchange tickled the show's loyal fans. *The Simpsons* began its twenty-fifth season in 2013.

The value of cartoons in our media diets may seem, at first, to be questionable. Cartoons equate to mental junk food in the minds of many. "Perhaps because it reminds us of our childhood and Saturday mornings in front of the TV, we tend to see the medium of animation as unsophisticated," writes culture critic Jennifer McMahon.[2] A closer look at cartoons, though, reveals situations, characters, and themes that apply to real-world or serious issues confronting humankind. The medium has been used to teach young children values and skills (*Dora the Explorer* and *Blue's Clues*), to challenge a social status quo (*Ren & Stimpy*, *The Simpsons*, and *South Park*), and even, in the 1940s, to convince a nation to join a war in Europe and pay federal income taxes to buy military weapons for the battle (Disney's Donald Duck). Because of its cultural ubiquity, the role of cartoons in U.S. culture deserves serious attention.

An increasing number of scholars agree on the need to look carefully at cultural messages in cartoons. Communications scholar Douglas R. Bruce says that children's cartoons are like nursery rhymes; their messages can help us better understand our world.[3] In the book *Media Virus: Hidden Agendas in Popular Culture* (1994), media scholar Douglas Rushkoff points out that because people don't suspect that cartoons might have any impact at all on culture, themes and messages that might undermine the accepted norms of a society often fly under the radar.

Rushkoff describes the "innocuous veneers" of cartoons as a kind of disguise that lets cartoon creators address some serious or controversial topics. A simple cartoon like *Rocky and Bullwinkle* serves as a "satire of America's cold war paranoia," and Bart Simpson represents America's youth with his savvy approach to media and willingness to question taboos.[4] "I find you can get away with all sorts of unusual ideas if you present them with a smile on your face," says Matt Groening, creator of *The Simpsons*.[5]

Of course, just because cartoons may possess embedded messages intended for unsuspecting viewers does not mean those embedded messages are always honest, independent, or productive. A critic recognizes that animation has also been used as a tool by the persuasion industries and evaluates cartoons on an individual basis—just like books, music, or newspapers—looking for those that better meet her information and entertainment needs.

Animation's History—A Sketch

When a person mentions cartoons, the first that come to mind might be colorful kiddie animations—*Mickey Mouse, Road Runner, Scooby Doo, SpongeBob,* or *Dora the Explorer.* But, as noted above, more mature animation has made its way into prime-time and cable television over the past 20 years. Think cartoons like *South Park,* which uses crude language and dark humor to satirize a variety of topics. Animation has also become a staple of the movie industry. Movies that qualify as animations—that use computer-generated imagery to make up a large chunk of the movie's frames—dominate the list of all-time top 25 blockbuster movies (rated by profits). The list includes

Marvel's *The Avengers, Iron Man 3, Transformers: Dark of the Moon, Harry Potter and The Deathly Hallows Part 2,* and *Toy Story 3*—all watched by millions in the United States and around the globe.

In the early 1900s, animation was in its infancy. Some of its earliest artists came from print journalism, where they drew popular comic strips for newspapers.[6] A short film recorded in 1900 by Thomas Edison might qualify as one of the first animations. The film records live action of a newspaper cartoonist James Stuart Blackton as he draws a smiling face and various objects on a large white pad. Because the director stopped filming at planned intervals, Blackton appears to pluck an actual bottle and glass from the paper. For early cartoons, artists drew all individual pictures or frames by hand.

An animated feature nowadays involves artists working on computers to generate hundreds of thousands of individual frames via CGI, or computer-generated imagery. For *The Hobbit* (2012), director Peter Jackson created a film that contained 48 frames per second. Since the film ran 169 minutes, the movie contained nearly half a million individual frames.

Also, though computerized imagery is now used for most of *The Simpsons*, the show's makers still brag about the rough appeal of the work, going so far as to say "ugly and two-dimensional" in a trailer for *The Simpson's Movie*.[7] "I love the crude, hand-drawn line," series creator Matt Groening told a reporter. "It's not perfect, but you can see the humanity in it. CGI animation, when it's not done with the wit and style of those films, is cold and airless."[8]

In *The Simpsons*, characters are drawn simply with large oblong heads, round eyes, and only four fingers. The characters are colored an unnaturally bright yellow. That factor might have helped the family gain global appeal because audiences from many ethnic backgrounds might identify with the characters. In fact, many U.S. cartoons, from Disney movies to *The Simpsons*, are translated into a dozen languages, re-recorded with new voices in Spanish or Italian, and shown around the globe. This international export of American culture gives us another reason to look at the HIP factor of cartoons, to ask questions about the honesty, independence, and productivity of funny and fantastical animated worlds.

Cartoons, Honest?

Honesty seems an unlikely value to expect from a cartoon. Cartoons create impossible fantasies, transporting audiences into imaginative realms where anything can happen. In iconic Warner Brothers *Road Runner* cartoons, Wile E. Coyote dies a thousand deaths—usually the result of faulty application of his own road runner–hunting inventions. In the much newer Cartoon Network's *Adventure Time*, a human boy pairs with his best friend—a talking, shape-shifting dog. Dog and boy battle an inventive group of monsters and mutants in a surreal environment that seems a mix of the game Candy Land with the post-apocalyptic movie classic *Mad Max*.

Nothing seems real about the characters or the settings of many animated shows. But, as noted with parody news, honesty does not always take the form of literal truth. A fictitious world—like those created by cartoons—can offer a useful place to explore deeper "truths" about everything from family relationships to business practices to political and social issues.

That's an argument that media scholar Jennifer McMahon makes about cartoons in her essay "The Function of Fiction."[9] Some realities about how our world works are communicated best through a fictitious tale, she writes. In considering *The Simpsons*, McMahon suggests that audiences find authenticity in the mundane conflicts of a middle-class suburban family with a dysfunctional dad Homer, practical though self-deluded mom Marge, and 2.5 kids (Bart, Lisa and Baby Maggie who doesn't speak). *The Simpsons* allows viewers to identify with the "commonplace" inhabitants and institutions of a city called "Springfield," vaguely located somewhere in the United States. McMahon writes: "Of course, if truths cannot be ordinary, then *The Simpsons* might not offer much. However, it seems that oftentimes it is the ordinary truths that elude us."[10]

What are some of these "ordinary" moments of authenticity in *The Simpsons*? Fans recite the truths they've learned from the show. Vegetarians say they were inspired by the example of Lisa Simpson. The faithful monogamy of Homer and Marge—though occasionally challenged—has been portrayed in moving ways over 25 years and inspires couples to fall in love all over again. In "Everything I Need To Know, I Learned From the Simpsons," pop culture blogger Jessica Tholmer lists as a favorite lesson: "Siblings are our most important asset," she writes, noting that two episodes of *The Simpsons* made her cry—in one, Lisa and Bart make up after a long fight and, in another, Bart sucks it up and sings to Lisa.[11]

Viewers can also relate to the community in which the Simpsons live, whose leaders are often clueless, where a wealthy businessman, Mr. Burns, wields a huge amount of power, and the school operates with a charming degree of absurdity. The most influential community gathering venues appear to be the church and Moe's Tavern. In feature-length *The Simpsons Movie*, when the town is threatened with impending apocalypse, a scene depicts people flooding out of both the church and bar. These folks look into the sky—and then switch places. The churchgoers heading into the bar and the drinkers going to church. The comic moment seems, to the show's audience, an apt observation of human behavior.

Do all cartoons offer up, as fiction, honest representations of reality? Of course not. Cartoons have been used as political propaganda, as commercial advertisements, and as motivational tools. The thing to remember here is that the possibility exists for colorful fantasy cartoon worlds to offer something authentic—that honest is not out of the question.

Cartoons, Independent?

Like other media, the ability of cartoons to offer information or access to "truths" in an independent way most often depends on who is paying to produce the media. As noted above, a cartoon can have an agenda or a bias. Most often this happens when an animation is crafted with some type of persuasive goal.

Since the early days of animation, governments have hired cartoonists to create promotional tools that would be widely disseminated. Soviet Union–era propaganda made before and during the cold war (1940s–1980s) included animations that showed capitalism as exploitation of the workers and that exposed U.S. hypocrisy on race relations.[12] At the same time, animations in the United States promoted the benefits of capitalism. "Make Mine Freedom," shows young people dancing in malt shops and thriving under an industrious system of privately owned businesses, a system in which people work hard to become successful.[13]

Animator Walt Disney's cartoons of the 1930s–1950s provide interesting examples of challenges to cartoon independence. Disney's first cartoons were artful works based on fairy tales and children's books. By the 1930s, Walt Disney had made the first feature-length animation, *Snow White and the Seven Dwarfs* (1937). But Disney's next three feature animations—*Pinocchio, Fantasia,* and *Bambi*—all failed at the box office, leaving Disney owing millions to the Bank of America. Things might not have gone as well for the company if not for the U.S. entry into World War II and Disney's contracts with the U.S. government to make films for at least six agencies. By 1942, about 90 percent of Disney's 550 employees were at work "making films that bear directly on the war," reported *Life* magazine.[14]

Disney's beloved Donald Duck was rolled out to tout the benefits of paying federal income taxes in "The New Spirit"[15] and mocked Adolf Hitler in "Der Fuehrer's Face."[16] At one point, the animator felt compromised by having to use his all-American duck to channel the military's message. "Disney was said to have referred to his beloved character as a captive," writes Disney biographer Marc Eliot, "forced to perform like little Pinocchio."[17]

It's not hard to see a bias in government-financed animation. Less obvious, though, are the partialities of media that cater to popular demand. Disney's short cartoons created for various U.S. government agencies seem much different from the company's contemporary animated features produced by Disney's distribution company Buena Vista, movies that include *Lion King*, the *Toy Story* trilogy, *Finding Nemo,* and the third-highest box office money-maker of all time, Marvel's *The Avengers.*[18] These movies seem much more independent in their choice of content and themes. What might limit the independence of a blockbuster animation?

The independence of a cartoon's content may be dictated by what the media corporations know consumers want. That's not censorship—but it isn't exactly independence either.

Less concerned about what gains a wide public appeal, perhaps, are animators Trey Parker and Matt Stone, creators of *South Park.* The animators say they eschew any allegiance to any social, political, religious, or philosophical point of view in their long-running Comedy Central cartoon, making a claim for the show's independence. The cartoon has been notable for being foul-mouthed and merciless in its mockery. Episodes are crafted around the misadventures of four elementary school-aged boys who cuss frequently, fixate on bodily functions—and confront big ideas and serious issues in unexpected ways. Often the show's plot is built around current social and political events. Past episodes have addressed race relations, Pres. Barak Obama's reelection, the overuse of Facebook, and institutionalized approaches to school bullying.

Parker and Stone boast about their independence—and their ability to offend just about everyone with their content. Critics of the show include liberals, conservatives, environmentalists, women, parents, educators, Roman Catholics, Scientologists, Mormons, Baptists, atheists, and those Hollywood actors mocked on a regular basis, including Alec Baldwin and Tom Cruise.

A parody so honest that it makes just about everyone uncomfortable? That just might be the key to artful, democratic independence.

Cartoons, Productive?

In the first five minutes of the *Dora the Explorer* episode "Puppies Galore," a pre-kindergarten audience encounters a bilingual learning moment while discussing canine hygiene. For the dirty puppies, it's "bath time" in English or "*a bañarse*" in Spanish. The audience is asked to repeat these words and given time to do so. Later, a song about maps reminds young people that they can find directions to places they'd like to go. The characters count puppies and doggie treats—doing simple math problems. Dora gives 12 puppies a bath and one disappears. That leaves 11 puppies. The importance of taking a bath—or at least of keeping puppies clean—is reiterated a couple of times, too, simply teaching hygiene. The children and animals are polite and kind, cooperating to solve problems.[19] The content is unabashedly educational.

Educators use cartoons to teach young children and to expose teens and adults to new perspectives. As we've seen from the use of cartoons as government propaganda, the medium has been used as a persuader and to influence attitudes and behavior.

Do cartoons work? In the 1940s, Disney's Donald Duck proved to be an effective way to promote the federal income tax. A World War II–era Gallup poll commissioned by the U.S. Treasury Department to determine the Disney cartoon's effectiveness observed that about 60 million Americans saw the film and that support for federal income taxes had increased by 37 percent.[20]

Promoting a different cause, Canadian animator John Kricfalusi inserted subversive and controversial comedy about the sexual preferences of central characters in the children's cartoon *Ren & Stimpy* (1991–1996). "I think we are destroying the minds of America," Kricfalusi once told journalists, "and that's been one of my lifelong ambitions."[21] Although the animator's comment seems almost hostile, his goal seemed not to destroy but to enable a wider understanding and acceptance of a progressive agenda. The show is merely one of several TV programs in the past two decades that have promoted acceptance of gay and lesbian lifestyles. So, few were surprised when, in 2013, a Pew Research poll found the millennial generation (born in 1981 or later) expressed the highest levels of support for same-sex marriage. Support for same-sex marriage has been going up consistently for much of the last decade.[22]

The educational value of a cartoon isn't limited to its content, Jennifer McMahon suggests. The form of animation deserves to be considered by itself as a productive medium. Unlike a live-action TV drama, a cartoon character drawn in bold outlines with, say, a giant blue hairdo like Marge Simpson, isn't going to be mistaken for a "real" character.

"Through their form, animated works offer us a powerful reminder that we are not the characters with whom we identify," McMahon writes.[23] Thus, the audience can reflect more deeply on the characters' actions, the situations in which they find themselves, and their feelings and thoughts.

So cartoons teach. They influence us. They help us experience reality through their unreality. They have mass appeal. Like any media tool, if these characteristics are used in honest and independent ways, they'll be marvelously productive in making us more thoughtful participants in our culture and in making us, ultimately, better ancestors.

BE THE CRITIC

- Watch several of Disney's World War II–era animations that were funded by the Canadian and U.S. governments. Recommended: "All Together" (1941), "The New Spirit" (1942), and "Education for Death: The Making of the Nazi" (1943). All are available as free downloads at the Internet Archive, https://archive.org.

- Describe the details of the animations. What ideas and attitudes are being taught by these cartoons? How does the animator convey these attitudes and ideas?

- Analyze the patterns in the cartoons. What characters appear and reappear? What moments are humorous? What ideas and arguments are not shown?

- Evaluate the cartoons for their usefulness as educational tools. What works—and what doesn't work? Can you tell the animation was funded by the government? What gives it away?

SATIATE YOUR CURIOSITY

- Watch some of the earliest animations online. The Library of Congress's version of "The Enchanted Drawing" is available at YouTube: http://www.youtube.com/watch?v=pe7HSnZotbU. "How a Mosquito Operates" by Winsor McCay (1912) is also on YouTube: http://www.youtube.com/watch?v=yvzAJouHh7k

- Read the interactive feature "The Simpsons Turn 25. Here Are Five Things They've Taught Us." This slideshow has some fun visuals, short readings, and links to various clips: http://fusion.net/culture/story/lessons-learned-simpsons-show-7795#.UcHy3oUoOTI

- A Disney website gives you a chance to make a flipbook of your own, using the help of computer imagery. http://disney.go.com/create/apps/flipbook

- Make your own animated video at an easy-to-learn website, Go Animate, http://goanimate.com

 # Sports Media

"[T]he playing field is where we can project our every thought, hope, and fear. We want to believe fiercely that this is the one place where ability alone determines how we are judged. If you can play, you will play, no matter your color, class, or gender."

—Dave Zirin, *A People's History of Sports in the United States*[1]

Perhaps nothing brings families in the United States together like Super Bowl Sunday. We feast on chips, carbonated beverages, chicken wings, and pizza. Together, families and friends gather around television screens, large and small, to watch the game. Even those not interested in the teams playing might join the party to watch the year's most clever advertising and enjoy the half-time show.

This annual festival of football in the United States did not happen by accident. Our national affection for Super Bowl Sunday has been fueled by sports media—from the promotions of the game's network sponsors to the journalism being done at news venues across the nation to countless websites with sports blogs, replay videos, scores, stats, standings, and sports-related merchandise.

Sports media are inextricably linked to our culture's celebration of health, athleticism, and competition. Local news venues might cover adolescent soccer games. A network TV station carries footage of the Ladies Singles Figure Skating Competition during the Olympics. Sports organizations like the National Football League hire teams of public relations experts to promote the game, to manage the image of coaches and players, and to develop strategies to build excitement about a sport via social media.

The sports media cycle can be a profitable one. In local newspapers and on television, photos and stories of young athletes increase audience loyalty—resulting in increased newspaper sales or a greater number of TV commercial sponsors. On a national scale, media venues like ESPN earn money from the sports organizations and from advertisers selling beer, chips, and deodorant to audiences of sports enthusiasts. Annually, the Super Bowl is the biggest marketing event in the United States, with sponsors paying millions on Super Bowl promotions. In 2013, Fox charged up to $4 million for a 30-second advertisement. Super Bowl Sunday is the top at-home party of the year, writes Peter Keating of *ESPN The Magazine*, bigger than New Year's Eve, Thanksgiving, or Christmas. "But financial stats tell only part of the story," Keating writes, noting that sales of big-screen TVs quintuple during Super Bowl week, more women watch the Super Bowl than the Academy Awards, and "nine of the 10 most-viewed programs in television history have ended with the presentation of the Lombardi Trophy."[2]

Whether or not she's a fan, a media critic needs to observe the impact of sports storytelling through mass media. As reporter Dave Zirin wrote in *A People's History of Sports in the United States*, the powerful political and cultural implications of our national obsessions as recorded by sports media cannot be ignored. A careful critic might uncover some dismaying realities and, at the same time, gain a new appreciation for the role of competitive events in our society.

By looking at the integral role that sports media have in telling the stories of sporting activities from football to tennis to golf, a media critic develops a better understanding of the honesty, independence, and productivity of sports media. Zirin writes: "If we challenge sports to be as good as they can be—a force to break down walls that divide us, a motor for inclusion—they can propel us toward a better world, a world worth playing in—and worth fighting for."[3] An honest, independent, and productive sports media rise to the challenge Zirin describes.

A Short History of Sports Media

Perhaps one of the earliest examples of sports media might have been the *Book of Sports,* written in 1618 by England's King James. The king gave approval to recreational sports like dancing, archery, leaping, and vaulting as healthful alternatives to hanging out in bars, drinking, and making "idle and discontented speeches." The king argued that a side benefit of sports was encouraging the kind of exercise that would help young men become physically fit—and eventually better soldiers. Zirin likens the king's reasoning to a similar saying by Pres. Dwight Eisenhower: "The true mission of American sports is to prepare young men for war."[4]

Media attention to sports shifted as media technologies changed, but it remained an integral part of any news media. In the early 1800s, U.S. magazine and newspaper editors discovered that they could earn new subscribers by covering, at first, English sports like cricket and then horse racing in some parts of the United States. By the late 1800s, during the Yellow Press era, sports coverage played a key role in newspaper circulation wars between Joseph Pulitzer and William Randolph Hearst. "The degree . . . that 'yellow journalism' was responsible for the sporting impulse of the 1880s and 1890s [due to] the influence of [Pulitzer's] *New York World* cannot be overestimated," writes John Betts, a sports media historian. "The battle for circulation was a torrid one."[5]

As new communication technologies developed, sports media shifted their attention, transferring audience loyalties to the sport best served by the medium. For example, the medium of radio turned out to be well-suited to cover baseball. While radio surged into use by the middle class with offerings like comedies, dramas, variety shows, news, and soap operas, broadcasts of sporting events made the medium a hit. New broadcasting stars emerged with talents suited to the world of sound. "[T]he ability to describe a baseball game became so well articulated, so able to communicate visual experience, that sportscasters could re-create a game in the studio with only the recorded roar of the crowd and sound of a bat hitting a ball needed to simulate a virtual event," writes Robert Kolker in his textbook, *Media Studies*.[6] As a result, radio coverage of baseball created a nation of devoted fans.

Then came television, and, in 1967, the made-for-TV extravaganza that is the Super Bowl. "Football and television have been ideal partners," wrote the former head of ABC Sports Roone Arledge in a 1966 *Sports Illustrated* article, "It's Sport, It's Money . . . It's TV."[7] Unlike baseball, the shape of the football field corresponds to that of the screen, Arledge wrote. "And the pace and rhythm of football create an instant aura of action. Everyone in baseball *walks* everywhere. In football, even when nothing is happening, there is the appearance of action. Guys *run*." That's just good TV, Arledge concluded.

In his book *Glued to the Set*, author Steven D. Stark also describes how football was ready-made for television. Games were played on Sunday afternoons, when families went on outings and spent time together. It wasn't hard to retrain working professionals—OK, men—to modify their lifestyles to accommodate a Sunday afternoon spent in front of a television set. Stark quotes *New York Times* columnist Robert Lipsyte who described Sunday football games as a "'socially acceptable way' for men to tune out women on Sunday afternoons."[8] Audiences turned on televised football and another cultural shift occurred, one that's resulted in a widening popularity gap between baseball and football in the United States.[9]

Now, more than 100 million people watch the Super Bowl annually in the United States, which, most years, makes the sporting event the most-watched program on television. That's why rates for commercial advertisements can reach $2 million for a 30-second spot. ESPN sports commentator Jeff MacGregor opines that the cultural center of the United States is not New York City, Washington, D.C., or even Hollywood. "It is wherever the Super Bowl is being played," he writes. "While you weren't looking, the NFL became our national metaphor for everything. . . , the measure of America—the cultural yardstick that helps us understand who we are as a nation—is football."[10]

Is the measure of America football? Or baseball? Or ice skating? Does our identity emerge from athletic programming offered up for our nation's consumption by mostly for-profit sports media organizations? What kinds of factors might complicate the messages of sports media? These are fair questions for an observer of sports media. And that is why a media critic needs to take a closer look at the honesty, independence, and productivity of sports media to better understand the role they play in constructing a national identity.

Honesty in Sports Media

In 1966, Roone Arledge said he worried about the fusion of television and sports. He feared the media's impact on sports through their coverage would lead to unquestioned boosterism of games—cheerleading without asking any difficult questions. Because TV networks paid so much money to get exclusive rights to broadcast games, Arledge noted, the result would be sports coverage that promoted games and athletes without doing honest, straightforward sports reporting.

"In recent years, by spending millions of dollars for the rights to sports events, television has become the biggest promoter in history, while, at the same time becoming the largest source of information," Arledge wrote in *Sports Illustrated*. "This sets up a basic ethical conflict that television will have to face soon. Is it going to be strictly an entertainment medium or is it deserving of journalistic stature?"[11] Arledge's question, asked half a century ago, is a useful starting point for sports media critics of any era—especially today when Arledge's concern about "millions of dollars" has multiplied exponentially to billions of dollars.

Can sports journalists be honest about their coverage given the pressures of the emphasis on profit? Many sports journalists have risen to the challenge of honest reporting, taking hard looks at everything from doping by bicycling superstars to animal mistreatment in horse racing. Here are just a few examples:

- Irish sports reporter David Walsh pursued the truth about seven-time Tour de France–winning bicyclist Lance Armstrong for 13 years. At the start, Walsh's suspicions that Armstrong was at the head of illicit program that supplied steroids, blood boosters, and other performance-enhancing substances to athletes were met with scorn and a nearly million-dollar lawsuit against his newspaper, the *Sunday Times*. In 2012, though, Armstrong was banned from the Tour de France after an investigation affirmed Walsh's reporting.

- The *New York Times* coverage of horse racing in 2012 revealed that 24 horses die each week on U.S. racetracks. Many more horses were injured. A series of articles exposed the drugging of horses and those horse trainers who had been disciplined for mistreatment. The report led to political change as racing commissions in many states reassessed how much medication was permissible for thoroughbred racehorses. Media scholar Bryan E. Denham writes that the *New York Times* stories also educated members of the sports media. After the articles ran, journalists at other large newspapers and TV stations referenced the material and launched reporting efforts of their own to educate the public about problems with the sport.[12]

- In their book, *Game of Shadows: Barry Bonds, BALCO, and the Steroids Scandal That Rocked Professional Sports* (2006), journalists Mark Fainaru-Wada and Lance Williams revealed the use of performance-enhancing drugs by San Francisco Giant Barry Bonds and Yankee Jason Giambi. Their reporting helped inform the public, reporters—and even a U.S. president about steroid use. "I think the story was hard for a lot of people," Fainaru-Wada said in an interview for the PBS documentary *News Wars*. "First of all, a lot of sports reporters in particular, and really reporters in general, were not educated about the notion of steroids." Fainaru-Wada and Williams met Pres. George W. Bush, a baseball fan, at a dinner for journalists who work at the White House. Bush told the reporters, "Well, you guys have done a service," Fainaru-Wada recounted the president's words. "He clearly knew what was going on, and he clearly told us the stories have done some good."[13]

For those who might fear that marketing forces might co-opt sports journalism, it's encouraging to see reporters like Fainaru-Wada and Williams seek out verifiable information. Fainaru-Wada told a *PBS Frontline* interviewer that he wanted to counter the message that drugs are handy ways to give an athlete a boost isn't lost on young sport stars in training. "That message is going to trickle down," Fainaru-Wada said. "There's no question. . . . The reality is these drugs are vastly more dangerous for young teenage boys in particular than they are for you or me."[14] That's the value of honest sports journalism.

Independence in Sports Media

Playing football for the New York Jets in 1999, tight end Kyle Brady took a helmet-to-helmet hit during a game. His vision blurred and he felt nauseated. "I wasn't aware of where I was," he later told ESPN reporters. A doctor took a look at Brady and sent him back into the game even though Brady couldn't remember plays and didn't know where to line up. "I don't think it was the right decision," he said. "It wouldn't have been the right decision to put anybody on the field to play that day."[15]

The doctor who made that decision, Elliot Pellman, was on the NFL's payroll. Dr. Pellman had led efforts to discredit independent medical research on head injuries. He was the lead author in 9 of 16 NFL-sponsored studies, "many of which suggested concussions were not a significant problem in the NFL," according to ESPN.[16] Was the doctor acting independently in making medical decisions and publishing medical journal articles that supported the NFL?

Peer-reviewed journals are often considered to be the most independent of media forms. Academic research, at its best, seeks accurate and verifiable information from scientific tests that are observed and repeated. This information may or may not serve the interests of a powerful organization like the NFL. But if the NFL paid for the research, the results might, perhaps, be looked at with a hearty helping of skepticism.

Independent journalism also seeks the truth even if it's not flattering or financially profitable to a large sports organization. Most sports journalists are not on the NFL's payroll, though through advertising and other paid promotions, the NFL's impact on large U.S. media companies shouldn't be overlooked. That said, a few sports journalists have done extensive investigations of head injuries in football and other sports, exposing some of the sports organizations' decisions that seemed not in the best interests of its players. That's an independent—and financially risky—move. It's not surprising that the most revealing reports on the NFL's handling of concussions came from the *New York Times* or ran on public television, which is arguably less influenced by the sport's league financial clout. More impressive is reporting done by sports journalists at ESPN, a sports network with plenty of financial interest in keeping the NFL popular.

In 2005, reporters from the *New York Times* and ESPN investigated Dr. Pellman's credentials when he testified for the National Baseball Association during a congressional investigation on steroid use. Dr. Pellman gave a glowing account of baseball's stringent safeguards against performance-enhancing drugs but didn't seem to understand the process of drug regulation.[17] The *Times* found discrepancies between Dr. Pellman's biographical statements and his job history.[18] The *Times* reporters were doing independent journalism.

Of course, reporters are only as independent as the news organizations for which they work allow them to be. In 2013, ESPN reporters were contributing to a PBS documentary about the NFL's handling of concussion. ESPN had even sponsored the documentary. Before the show aired, though, ESPN pulled out of its sponsorship.

How could this happen?

ESPN explained that the company realized, at the last minute, that it lacked editorial control over the documentary's content. Writing in *The Nation* magazine, Dave Zirin quoted an anonymous ESPN writer who, like many others, believed that the NFL had flexed its muscle and forced ESPN to toe its line. "Generally, ESPN's business interests will always be at odds with its journalism," the ESPN writer told Zirin. "It is not a journalism company. It's an entertainment company. This is the age of journalism we live in, not just at ESPN but everywhere. Journalism is increasingly more corporate. When you get in bed with the devil, sooner or later you start growing your own horns."[19]

Why might the NFL's demands be so important to ESPN? From advertising to merchandise, football's a huge moneymaker. Football content drives viewers and readers to ESPN's stations, websites, and publications. ESPN's parent company Disney, also, must maintain good relations with large companies that spend gigantic sums on marketing and promotions—and that have a large fan base. All these can limit media independence.

Although ESPN withdrew its support, the *PBS Frontline* documentary *League of Denial: The NFL's Concussion Crisis* aired on October 8, 2013, right in the middle of fall football season. ESPN's logo was not on the documentary or in the credits—though ESPN reporters and brothers Steve Fainaru and Mark Fainaru-Wada did much of the reporting. Shortly before the PBS documentary aired, the NFL settled a lawsuit with 4,500 former players, paying $766 million to help retirees whose brains had been damaged by concussions.

A physician lacking proper credentials was hired by the NFL to craft and publish medical research that didn't reflect real or useful information. That's not independent media content. Reporters acting independently investigated and exposed this. The sports network ESPN pulled its sponsorship from the concussion documentary but the program was completed, aired on public television, and is available online at PBS Frontline's website.

While the forces of a big business can flex their muscle to co-opt media messages, the sports journalist with a story to tell finds a way to tell it. That's independence.

Sports in the Media, Productive?

Author Stephen Dubner, who wrote *Confessions of a Hero Worshiper*, says he appreciates sports fandom because it's a stand-in for real life—with conflicts that seem real but, at the end of the game, are manufactured. "It's a war where nobody dies," Dubner said. "It's a proxy for all our emotions and desires and hopes."[20]

A war where nobody dies—that sounds productive. In what other ways might sports media be useful in making us better ancestors?

Sports media fuel the dreams of young athletes who want to compete, say, for a gold medal in the global sporting arena. Drawn to the images of athletes they see on TV and in newspapers, young people train hard to compete in the Olympics. Media representations motivate athletes. "I began at school, at the age of nine and, as my training progressed, I took part in competitions, achieving results until I gained recognition," says Sarah Menezes, a Brazilian athlete who competed in the 2008 Beijing games.[21]

The question of sports media productivity might begin with looking at the reasons we love sports media and the activities on which they report, celebrate, or offer challenges.

We are a nation of sports aficionados who enjoy playing and watching others play. Many of us revel in physical activities—including team sports, hiking, biking, swimming, and hula-hooping—that keep our bodies and minds healthier. Competitive sports build our capacity for strategy, and, in many cases, our abilities to work together as a team.

More than 7.6 million high school students participated in sports in the 2010–2011 school year, according to a U.S. Department of Health website, which also lists a few benefits of playing sports:

- Young people who participate in athletics enjoy lower rates of diabetes and high blood pressure.

- Athletes have better lung capacity and stronger hearts.

- Athletes have lower rates of obesity.

- Athletes are less likely to smoke cigarettes or use drugs.

- High school athletes have higher grade point averages, higher standardized test scores, better attendance, lower dropout rates, and a better chance of going to college.

- A survey of high-level executives at Fortune 500 companies showed that 95 percent of them played sports in high school.[22]

So it seems the celebration of athleticism by and through the sports media can be a positive force in our culture. Media outlets that cover sports—from local newspapers to websites to broadcast TV stations—can promote healthful athletics and can contribute to a productive conversation about the role of athletics in our society. Stories of athletic success inspire generations of young people to work hard to achieve their own dreams. The narrative of sports parallels our nation's cultural mythology—the belief that anyone who works hard can be successful and that luck has only a minor role.

Of course, like honesty and independence, the productivity of sports media needs to be put into some context. Let's look at the global phenomenon of the Olympics.

A media spectacle as much as an athletic event, the Olympics were intended by founder Pierre de Coubertin, a French aristocrat, to be a sporting event that would bring nations together. The global sporting event, through its media coverage, would promote the "ideal of a higher life" and offer every human an equal chance at success. The Olympics would celebrate "the springtime of mankind" and "glorify beauty by the involvement of the arts and the mind in the Games."[23]

Nowadays, the Olympics are a "powerful window for national and international politics," writes scholar Michele Acuto.[24] With the intense—and profitable—media spotlight on the games, massive media audiences are exposed to the connections between sports and politics, between athletics and diplomacy. Journalists and political leaders use the Olympics as a starting point for social commentary. The 2014 Winter Olympics in Sochi, Russia, became an occasion to make the rest of the world aware of Russia's "propaganda" law, which had been passed the previous year. The law bans the "promotion of homosexuality to minors" and news reports describe arrests of and fines for high school teachers, newspaper editors, activists—even a woman who started a social media page for gay teenagers.[25] Media reports were productive in raising awareness of the issue, though the *Washington Post* reported that after the Olympics, gays in Russia were feeling "more vulnerable than ever [under the] wrath of a repressive new law."[26]

Can sports media be a productive force for promoting gender equality for athletes? To celebrate female athletes with the same level of admiration and respect given to male athletes? While the potential certainly exists, reports suggest that sports media coverage isn't exactly rising to that challenge.

Women make up 38–42 percent of athletic participants, according to the Women's Sport Foundation (WSF). "Yet research indicates that sportswomen receive approximately 6–8 percent of the total sports coverage."[27] And, when women's sports are reported, sportscasters are more likely to comment on a woman's appearance or her emotional state, reinforcing stereotypes of women as cute sex objects who might cry if they don't win. "Images are powerful tools that shape and reflect attitudes and values," argues the WSF. "By portraying sportswomen either as sex objects or as 'pretty ladies,' the message is that sportswomen are not strong, powerful and highly skilled individuals."[28]

A study of 2012 Olympic coverage showed that, for the first time, women athletes received the majority of clock-time and on-air mentions during NBC's televised event coverage. "In an age where most televised sports are still a 'boys' club,' the Olympics are a relative anomaly, featuring a plethora of women athletes competing in virtually all the same sports as men."[29] The researchers qualified their findings, however, attributing the TV network's giving of more airtime to women to be largely the result of the focus on women's gymnastics and beach volleyball. They noted that gymnastics has been considered a gender-appropriate sport for women and that critics have challenged the sexualized nature of beach volleyball, "where women are often wearing tight-fitting bikinis."[30] Deep sigh.

On the bright side, the number of female athletes in the United States has risen exponentially in the past several decades. Every nation competing in the 2012 Olympic Games had at least one woman member—including, for the first time, Saudi Arabia, Qatar, and Brunei.[31] That seems a productive start.

BE THE CRITIC

- Observe your local TV news or read local newspaper coverage of sports for four or five weeks. Keep a list of the sports that get covered. How are these stories told? Write down some of the details you've observed in how reporters talk or write about sports. For example, are games described with the same kinds of language used to describe a military battle?

- Analyze the list. What patterns emerge in sports media? Are some sports covered more than others? Do you observe any consistencies in the language used to describe winning, losing, or the efforts by individual players?

- Interpret your findings. Why do you think some sports get more attention than others? What factors might underlie the way we talk (and think) about sports?

- Finally, evaluate your local sports media. What kinds of reporting are done well? What suggestions might you have for improvement? You may want to write a letter to a local sportswriter or TV reporter about your findings.

SATIATE YOUR CURIOSITY

- Back in 1966, Roone Arledge, the director of *ABC Sports,* wrote about the conflicting goals of sports media—journalism versus hype—in a *Sports Illustrated* article, "It's Sport, It's Money . . . It's TV." It's fascinating to read the article, archived at the magazine's website, now—some 50 years later. http://sportsillustrated.cnn.com/vault/article/magazine/MAG1078465/index.htm

- *The New Yorker's* Malcolm Gladwell offers an intriguing and controversial perspective on performance-enhancing drug use in his article "Man and Superman: In Athletic Competitions, What Qualifies as a Sporting Chance?" http://www.newyorker.com/arts/critics/atlarge/2013/09/09/130909crat_atlarge_gladwell

- Two useful documentaries look at concussions in sports. *Head Games: The Film* takes a broad look at concussions from professional sports right down to youth leagues, http://headgamesthefilm.com. *PBS Frontline's League of Denial* is an in-depth investigation of professional football, complete with video footage of brains damaged by repeated blows to the head. http://www.pbs.org/wgbh/pages/frontline/league-of-denial/

13 Hoaxes, Jokes, and Viruses

"For hundreds of years, humans have been playing elaborate tricks on each other, but the advent of social tools—from Usenet and email right on up to YouTube and Twitter—means that hoaxes are much more easily spread, and it can be difficult to separate the misinformation from the truth."

—Josh Catone, Mashable.com[1]

Friends and friends of friends post facts, assertions, misinformation, practical jokes, and outright lies on social networks sites, in blogs, in emails, photos (sometimes altered or "fauxtographs"), and shared videos. Cybercriminals offer deals that are too good to be true on sites like Craigslist. Crooks build fake login screens that look real for banks or PayPal or Facebook and use phishing methods to get you to type in your login information so they can take over your account. Strangers befriend you online—and you don't know, really, who they are or what kinds of motives they have for seeking out your friendship.

Sometimes it's hard to know what to believe, what information can be trusted to pass along or act on. To avoid looking silly, losing large sums of money, infecting your computer with malicious software, or getting involved in a sketchy relationship, a savvy Internet user needs to take the time to find out whether information and conversations online are accurate, verifiable, honest. That's the HIP thing to do.

For starters, a savvy media critic reposts nothing, shares no links, hits no "retweet" button if the information is in any way suspicious. If in doubt, don't repost. Remember, information—true and false, real and imagined—travels as fast as the speed of an Internet connection nowadays. Double-check everything. Look it up elsewhere. Let the lie stop with you. This advice will save tons of embarrassment—or worse, a lawsuit.

Learn from the shoddy example of American filmmaker Spike Lee, who passed along to his 256,000 Twitter followers a tweet with wrong information. Lee's tweet included the home address of George Zimmerman, the Florida man who killed an unarmed 17-year-old in 2012. That's some ethically sticky territory, for starters. By posting Zimmerman's address, Lee and others were inviting a kind of justice outside the court system. But the problem was compounded when, instead of Zimmerman's address, the address Lee retweeted was that of an elderly couple uninvolved in the controversy. This couple ended up receiving hate mail and threats of violence intended for Zimmerman. No fun, right? Lee apologized to the couple on Twitter and with a telephone call. He also paid them an undisclosed amount of money.[2]

Spike Lee's mistaken tweet turned into a nightmare for those involved. The incident hurt Lee's reputation and cost him money. But those are mild consequences compared with other forms of Internet scams or the lures of an online sex predator. Hoaxes and scams can cause victims to lose money or possessions.

In a few tragic cases, people have been lured into unsafe and even fatal situations by Internet predators who troll for victims through chat rooms, social networks, and classified advertising sites. A Texas man was arrested for luring victims to an apartment by offering free or cheap rent on Craigslist, then raping them. The classified ad website Backpage.com was linked to the murders of four women in Detroit, Michigan.

Online hoaxes and scams are the toxic waste of the information landscape. A media critic identifies troubling posts or too-good-to-be-true offers online and keeps her distance. The remainder of this chapter doesn't need to ask whether hoaxes are honest, independent, or productive. They aren't. Instead, here are some examples that will help you identify a wide range of crappy information—from the merely stupid to the potentially dangerous.

Email Hoaxes

Harry Potter—a bad influence on young people? Recruiting young people to become witches and wizards? That's what a satire news article in *The Onion* reported. Popular Harry Potter books, the fake story claimed, had led to an increase in occult practices among young people. The story quoted nonexistent sources. It was a joke. Not everyone was laughing, though, especially sincerely religious individuals who may have thought, mistakenly, that the story was true—thanks to a hoax email. The email quoted the fake article and warned parents about Potter and a diabolical plot to turn young people into an army for the forces of darkness.

The Harry Potter email, which ends with a request to forward the email to everyone you know, exemplifies harmless email spam that clogs people's inboxes. Hoaxes are untrue, often outdated, emails or social network posts with three notable elements: an attention-getting hook, an action point, and a threat. The Potter email's hook reels unsuspecting readers in with "evidence" that Harry Potter books are evil. The message has a call to action that urges recipients to distribute the misinformation to others. Its threat: if the recipient doesn't act now, more young impressionable children will become occultists.

In this category, also, are the emails that suggest good luck if a person forwards this email to 100 people—or bad luck if the email gets deleted. Emails that make claims about nasty computer viruses have been known to survive online for years—even after they've been proven false again and again. Often the emails have impressive technological lingo that makes them sound quite accurate. Don't buy it!

On the other hand, an email from the technology guru at your school is going to be legit. She won't ask you for personal information—like your password. She won't suggest that you forward a message to all your contacts.

Phishing

You receive an email from your bank or credit card or PayPal or Amazon. Something's wrong with your account. You are asked to login with your password to verify purchases or access. The email, however, is not from your bank, credit card, PayPal or Amazon. The email sends you to an official looking website—one that is, in fact, quite fake. You enter your login and password, which is recorded by the phishers, who now have access to your bank, credit card, or PayPal account. Not good.

Phishing can happen by phone or direct mail, as well. Before you give any personal information or social security numbers or account information, know exactly who you're talking to.

Buying Online

If it sounds too good to be true . . . yes, you're getting the idea. Here's an example of a scam ad posted to Craigslist with a picture of an expensive sports utility vehicle for sale:

> Hi, I am selling my GMC Yukon Denali because my platoon has been sent back to Afganistan [sic] and don't want it get old in my backyard. The price is low because I need to sell it before November 16th. It has no damage, no scratches or dents, no hidden defects. It is in immaculate condition, meticulously maintained and hasn't been involved in any accident . . . I do have the title, clear, under my name. The vehicle has 35,000 miles and here's its vehicle identification number.

> It is still available for sale if interested, price as stated in the ad $4,300. The car is in Baltimore, MD, in case it gets sold I will take care of shipping. Let me know if you are interested, email back. Regards!!!

Yes, the seller misspelled Afghanistan. But misspelled words can happen in legitimate posts. The seller appears to have given the potential buyer detailed information about the car, including the Vehicle Identification Number.

What makes a savvy online shopper suspicious? First, the sympathetic identity of the seller—we trust soldiers and missionaries!—plus the low, low asking price for a low-mileage vehicle that's free of defects. And free shipping! What a deal! The SUV—a slick vehicle offered at an irresistible price—is bait. By using Kelley Blue Book's online calculator that estimates used car values, I can see the vehicle is worth at least four times the asking price. A new Denali's running around $58,000. So, the deal seems too good to be true. That should set off your alarms.

The victim is the person who believes she can have this fabulous car for cheap, cheap. What might happen with this scam? The buyer might be asked to deposit money into a fake or fraudulent escrow service. Or the seller might asker the buyer to wire money via Western Union, Money-Gram, or another legitimate money transfer service. The seller assures the buyer that the money can't be accessed until the buyer receives the goods and passes along a Money Transfer Control Number or confirmation code. That feels safe, right? Wrong. "This is FALSE," warns the About Scams content at Craigslist. "Once you've wired money, it is GONE."[3]

In yet another scam, the buyer might ask for a partial payment up front—kindly noting that he trusts the buyer to pay the rest when the goods are delivered. So, the buyer sends half the asking price, in this case, $2,150. The Denali never arrives. The soldier and the vehicle didn't exist except as the inventions of a con artist, who promises the vehicle is on its way. Then the fraudster simply disappears with the dough.

Selling Online

The same scams can apply when you sell online, only in reverse. Con artists are skilled at printing fake cashier's checks and money orders. These look real to you—and even to the bank teller who deposits them into your account. The fake might not be discovered for a week or more. And then guess who is responsible to pay the bank back? You are.

Few fraudsters, however, actually want your stuff. Most want money. One way to get money from a person who's selling, say, a legacy Super Nintendo Entertainment System with 124 games, is to send a cashier's check or money order for more than the asking price—and then request a refund. The seller sends the refund before she finds out that the cashier's check or money order is fake.

In one example from Craiglist's list of scams, a con artist acts as a go-between for an overseas client who wants to buy an $800 bike. The scammer explains that the bike seller will receive a certified check for $4,000. The bike seller is instructed to keep $800 for the bike and send $3,000 back to the seller via Western Union. The seller should keep the extra $200 for his trouble. How thoughtful! Until the check is discovered to be a fake—and the bike seller is out $3,000—and possibly his bike.

Online Romance

He's cool—an online big brother, at first. The teen girl can talk to him about anything. He says he's 22 years old and she believes him. He knows what kind of music she listens to, what games she plays, and what celebrity gossip amuses her. When she gets in a fight with friends or parents, he's there. He takes her side. Although she's never met him, the man she met online has become her best friend and most trusted confidant.

Of course, as she becomes closer to this man, he's going to want to take the relationship to what he calls "the next level." He'll ask her to do things, watch things, photograph things that might make her uncomfortable. Before long, he may want to meet her. That makes sense, right? Two people who care about each other should see each other face-to-face.

He arranges a meeting for the two of them. Should she go? When she hesitates, perhaps, he convinces her that he loves her. Or, in other cases, he threatens to tell her parents what she's been doing online—with him. Does the promise of romance or the threat of blackmail work? She doesn't want to lose her friend. Or her parents will be furious if they find out. She agrees to meet this young man, who may turn out to be a bit older and lots nastier than she had expected.

Welcome to the world of the sex predator skillfully lurking on social networks, in chat rooms, and on online gaming sites. The sex predator seeks young people—male and female, befriending them, offering gifts and, more important, a listening ear. The goal? Sexual activity online—and possibly offline.

While most offline sex predators pursue victims under age 12, researchers find that the victims of online child molesters are between the ages 13 and 17.[4] These victims aren't clueless kids. Most use the Internet in sophisticated ways and perhaps consider themselves more knowledgeable than some adults about online interactions. Most young people today know better than to give out personal information to a stranger they met in an online chat or game forum. But some young people do it anyway. About 5 percent of young people, researchers found, will talk about sex with a stranger online.

The victims of online sex predators have some common characteristics. They're more likely to have parental problems and to feel sad, depressed, or lonely. Many have histories of sexual abuse and most are willing to take the risks associated with online "romance"—in order to experience the reward of feeling loved and wanted.[5]

That said, if an online friendship is making you feel uncomfortable, tell someone you trust. Do it right now. This book can wait.

Scams and Fraud

Whether you're looking for a job or trying to sell a used video game system, computer networks have become indispensable. Buying and selling items online at sites like eBay and Craigslist can be lucrative for computer users. Many employers post legitimate jobs online and expect future employees to apply via the Internet. But, like everything, not all offers are exactly what they seem.

Job posts offering users a chance to work from home can be scams that quickly separate hopeful workers from what's left of their savings. Items are offered for sale that don't even exist. And that dream apartment rental? Folks have been known to collect deposits and rent on places they don't own—then disappear with your dough.

On its website, Craigslist offers hoax-spotting advice for its users. Its first and most important rule: "Deal locally with folks you can meet in person. Follow this one rule and avoid 99 percent of scam attempts."[6] Here's another important thing to remember: Craigslist does not "guarantee" any transactions or any users. So, if a posting on its site claims that Craigslist has researched the user and given him a stamp of approval, consider that a dead giveaway for fraud.

Here are a few common scams:

- **Nigerian/Ghana millionaire needs you**

    You are contacted by a wealthy foreigner who needs your help in moving his massive fortune—millions of dollars!—from an African nation. For your help, you will receive a percentage of his dough—millions of dollars! Sounds like a win-win, right? The author of this email or direct mail letter or classified ad is not asking you for any money. Not yet. As with all scams, if it sounds too good to be true, it probably is. As you begin to correspond with this rich human from Nigeria or Ghana, details unfold. Cash is needed for a bribe. Your bank account information is needed to make a deposit. You think, "What's $500 or even $5,000 when I'm going to be a millionaire soon?" But you aren't going to be a millionaire. After the con artists have deluded you with promises and soaked you for every dime, they'll disappear, leaving you broke but smarter. You won't get your money back—ever.

    You can avoid losing your money and get smarter now.

- **Rental property scam**

  You're searching the Internet classifies for an apartment to live in while you go to college in a state far from home. Looking at photos, you find the perfect place and the rent seems so, so low. You send an email to the owner, who maybe writes back from West Africa, where she's a missionary. Before you know it, you've sent this person a deposit and maybe even first and last month's rent. When you arrive at your new home, you discover that it doesn't exist. Or it doesn't belong to the person to whom you sent money. You've been scammed.

  Many variations of this scheme exist. For those dubious would-be renters, the West African missionary might simply ask to check your credit. This means sending along all your bank account and credit card information, along with your social security number and whatever else the fraudster needs to steal your identity and your dough.

  In a trickier scenario, the fraudster asks you to deposit money via Western Union to something called an escrow account—which could be a safe place to put money. This soothes you, a savvy Internet user who knows better than to just send a cashier's check overseas. Unfortunately, though the escrow account information looks real, it's fake—and you've lost your money.

- **Ticket scams**

  Yes, you can find bargain tickets to a concert or cheap plane tickets online. But plenty of opportunity for fraud exists here, too. The simplest scam involves selling fake tickets that look real to website users. By the time the event rolls around and the buyer finds out his ticket is a useless fake, the online seller has disappeared. With plane tickets, a fraudster might purchase real tickets, show these to the buyer via email—or even make arrangements to meet in person—and make the sale. After the sale, the fraudster returns the tickets for a refund. When the buyer shows up at the airport, she finds her ticket has been canceled. Her money's gone and she's stuck at the airport, hoping to fly stand-by.

If you want to buy tickets online, know how to do the needed research. Call or visit the concert venue or airline to make sure the tickets are real. To help prove that the initial transaction was authentic, ask the seller for receipts. Get the details of the deal in writing, including complete contact information for the seller—name, address, occupation, phone number, references. Verify that these details are accurate. If you're dealing with a con artist, these requests might make him drop you like a hot potato. That's a good thing, by the way. You have saved yourself the pain of showing up at the long-awaited, sold-out music festival with an invalid ticket. Nice work!

- **Fake jobs**

If it sounds too good to be true, it probably is. The dream job of being a nanny or au pair for a rich family? Could happen. But beware of any weird financial transactions. Did the family send a check for way more than a salary advance? One common scam involves sending a check or money order that appears real to the young person who thinks he's gotten the job. He cashes the check, using money to pay himself and sending the rest back to the family who hired him. This happens fast, before the check actually clears. When the check doesn't clear, the victim owes his bank the amount of the entire check—plus fees for a bounced check. He's also out all the money he sent back to the scammer. And, though it now may seem the least of his problems, he's also still unemployed.

- **Work-at-home pyramid schemes**

  If it sounds too good to be true, it probably is. You can make a gazillion dollars a month in the comfort of your own home. You'll be selling some obscure product or service (from soap to Internet connections) via social networks, email, and websites. It's easy. Call now.

  Work-at-home schemes sound great, but here's how the scam works. You sign up for employment. Maybe you'll attend a short seminar or job interview in a hotel room or online. At some point, you'll be asked for money. Your satisfaction will be guaranteed, of course. So you pay $19.99 or $199.99 or $19,999.99 for a starter's kit or an introductory workshop or initial investment that teaches you how to, basically, recruit others to pay $19.99 or $199.99 or $19,999.99 to the company. When you recruit someone, you get a portion of what that person pays. Then that person begins to recruit others, getting a portion of what they pay.

  The pyramid eventually collapses, obviously, as no real product or service is being offered. The folks who get in on the top levels make out like bandits. Woe to those who never see their $19.99 or $199.99 or $19,999.99 again. Your satisfaction, it turns out, was not really guaranteed.

- **Facebook "send money" scam**

  Using the "phishing" technique to trick you into revealing your user name and password, a cyber-criminal logs into your account. Pretending to be you—and in trouble—the criminal sends out a plea for help to your friends. The messages look personal and include a sad story about you being stuck in another city or country without any money or resources. The money that your friends send to help you ends up in the crook's bank account. If you think someone's gained access to your Facebook account and is sending out scam messages from it, you can fix the problem at Facebook Help Center's "Scams" page. https://www.facebook.com/help/344403945636114

BE THE CRITIC

- Visit Snopes.com and read through a list of email hoaxes. Pick one that intrigues you and do a closer study.

- Read the hoax email and determine how much of it is true. Is it based on a real story? Dig a little to find out where the hoax departs from reality.

- Identify the key parts of the hoax. Is there an attention-getting hook? An action plan? A threat?

- Read the Snopes entry about the hoax. Try to discern what about this hoax made it "sticky," that is, why unsuspecting computer users continued to forward the misinformation to all their friends.

- Decide what kinds of things you'll forward to friends or what links you'll post to a social network site. That's the action plan of this book. The only real threat is this: thinking before linking will save you the embarrassment of passing along hoaxes.

SATIATE YOUR CURIOSITY

- A site created by the Federal Bureau of Investigation offers tips and stories to keep consumers prepared for a variety of computer-related cons. "Getting educated and taking a few basic steps may well keep you from becoming a victim of crime and fraud," site content advises, "and save you a great deal of time and trouble." http://www.fbi.gov/scams-safety

- To keep clear of Craigslist scams, check out a useful article from *PC World*, in which the author states: "From garden-variety pyramid schemes to complex money laundering ploys to pet frauds, the sheer diversity of ways to get stiffed on Craigslist is unmatched." http://www.pcworld.com/article/188584/keep_clear_of_craigslist_scams.html

- Arm yourself with information so you don't fall victim to scam artists. Start by tracking stories at this website aptly named for the wise advice: "Remember, if it looks too good to be true, it probably is!" http://www.lookstoogoodtobetrue.com

- Check out a *Reader's Digest* profile of the wife-husband team of Barbara and David Mikkelson who run an award-winning myth-debunking website, Snopes.com. At the site, the couple battles the forces of virus warnings, urban legends, "fauxtography," and "glurges"—sweet stories sent via email or social media that urge reader to pass along to as many people as possible. http://www.rd.com/home/rumor-detectives-true-story-or-online-hoax/

Conclusion: That's a Wrap

Media literacy gets media consumers in the habit of looking for honesty, independence, and productivity in media. But really, that's just a beginning. On plenty of topics, we've merely scratched the surface. A media critic could take any of the topics covered in previous chapters and turn it into its own entire book—or volume of books. As noted, this book covers some basics and uses some specific examples. You might want to go into more depth in an area that interests you.

A few topics were addressed briefly that deserve closer attention. Thankfully, many great resources exist to fill in these gaps. Here are three important aspects of media literacy for you to explore next:

News Literacy

What is journalism and how is it changing? Who decides what gets to be on the index page of a news media website or gets highlighted on a cable news network? Many scholars have studied news media in depth. The Stony Brook University School of Journalism runs the Center for News Literacy, http://www.centerfornewsliteracy.org, which gives students the skills to gauge the "reliability and credibility" of news media.

Visual Literacy

How does an image work to communicate an idea or argument? Folks who study visual literacy learn to read pictures, photographs, caricatures, and infographics in the same way that others study print or broadcast texts. Guidelines for what you should know to be visually literate were drafted by the American Library Association. You can find them here: http://www.ala.org/acrl/standards/visualliteracy.

Code Literacy

How does computer software end up shaping the media messages to which we are exposed? An individual with computer programming code literacy begins to understand how a social network works—as a business, not just as a facilitator of human interaction. Media critic and author Douglas Rushkoff makes an argument that developing code literacy gives us a better chance of learning how to navigate digital environments without having to blindly accept the rules and limitations imposed by those who understand programming code. Read Rushkoff's essay on code literacy here: http://www.edutopia.org/blog/code-literacy-21st-century-requirement-douglas-rushkoff.

Appendix A: On Beyond Google—For Research

The teacher assigns a research paper, handing you a list of acceptable topics. You pick the topic that sounds most interesting, get online, and type key words into a Google search engine. Your search yields news articles, a Wikipedia entry, and several blogs on your chosen topic.

What can you use in your research paper? Before you start gathering facts about your research topic, it's important to look at the sources for your information. Any poorly educated or poorly informed dude with Internet access can blog about your topic. You can't trust everything you read online. (See Chapter 13 on Internet hoaxes for more on this.)

What websites are best to use for academic research? Government websites can provide statistics and facts. You'll recognize a government website by the telltale .gov extension in its URL.

Reliable news media can provide up-to-date information. The *New York Times, Washington Post, Chicago Tribune, Los Angeles Times*, and your hometown newspaper can be cited as sources for your research. As a savvy media critic, you know that newspapers aren't infallible. So it's a good idea to fact check the facts offered by journalistic venues whenever possible.

When evaluating online information, ask a few basic questions:

- Who is publishing this information? An organization or individual? Does he or she have the authority or expertise to offer opinions?

- Where was the information published? Anyone can craft a blog in 10 minutes using tools like Wordpress. Similarly, anyone can post wrong information to Facebook or Twitter in seconds. Better sources: a blog running at the *New York Times* website has at least been vetted by an editor. An article written by a reporter and running at the *Washington Post* website has been thoroughly edited and fact-checked. *Note: Use Wikipedia with awareness. The everyone-edited Wikipedia can give a reasonable overview of a subject— but since it can be amended by anyone, it may also contain wrong or out-of-context information. That's why some teachers balk at citing Wikipedia as your source. Instead, use Wikipedia's list of citations—news stories and government or education websites as a launchpad for your research. As always, double- and triple-check everything you find.*

- Why is the information being published? Is the resource purely informational or does the organization or individual seem to be promoting an agenda? Does the source have a bias, a political or social perspective about which you should be aware?

- Also, when was the information published? If there's a chance that it might be outdated, you'd better double-check. A news media story published in 2008 about a country in the Middle East, for example, might be woefully out-of-date about the country's current political status, which may have changed in dramatic ways over the past few years.

To get you started, I've listed a few of the sources that I used when researching this book on media literacy.

Primary Sources

American Library Association
http://www.ala.org/rusa/sections/history/resources/pubs/usingprimarysources

At its site, Using Primary Sources on the Web, The American Library Association's Reference and User Services Association offers detailed suggestions on finding, evaluating and citing primary sources on the web.

Government Websites

Federal Government
http://www.usa.gov

A portal to every federal government website.

State Governments
http://www.usa.gov/Agencies/State-and-Territories.shtml

The list on this website takes you to the state government's website for each state, as well as the District of Columbia and U.S. territories.

Online Newspapers

Many news media now maintain websites with searchable archives, including the *Washington Post* (http://www.washingtonpost.com) and the *Los Angeles Times* (http://www.latimes.com). One of the most thorough compilations of more than 100 years of U.S. news media lives at the *New York Times*. Information is sorted by topic at Times Topics. http://www.nytimes.com/pages/topics/index.html. The website includes an alphabetical listing of places, people, and topics in the news. The frequently updated site listings offer introductory information as well as links to past and current news articles.

Web Resources

Al Jazeera English
http://america.aljazeera.com

World news, analysis, and information, archived and searchable.

BBC
http://www.bbc.com

World news and information, archived and searchable, from the new venue formerly known as British Broadcasting Company.

Central Intelligence Agency World Factbook
https://www.cia.gov/library/publications/the-world-factbook/

The CIA's World Factbook includes profiles of 267 countries, nations, and/or world entities. The profiles offer reliable information on each entity's history, government, economy, geography, communications, transportation, and military. If you look up Libya, you'll find up-to-date information about the country's leaders—even if elections were held mere weeks ago.

Columbia Journalism Review
http://www.cjr.org/resources/

The publication's website includes "Who Owns What," an up-to-date database of media corporations and the properties and subsidiaries that each one owns. This is an invaluable resource for a media critic. The site also offers student study guides, links to research, and reports on the state of the media.

Crocodyl Collaborative Research on Corporations
http://www.crocodyl.org

The Crocodyl website offers a compilation of research and findings about large corporations. Material comes from other watchdog groups, including Center for Corporate Policy, CorpWatch, Corporate Research Project, other contributing organizations and individual contributors from around the world. Some of the entries are kept more up-to-date than others, so watch out for old info. "Crocodyl can help them challenge the public relations machines of big business by providing an easy-to-access snapshot of information about these companies, including an inventory of their misdeeds."

Fact Check and Flack Check

http://www.factcheck.org
http://www.flackcheck.org

As projects of the Annenberg Public Policy Center of the University of Pennsylvania, these sites operate as a fact-verification site and its political literacy companion site.

Internet Movie Database

http://www.imdb.com

IMDB.com is considered an authoritative source for information about movies, TV shows, and entertainment personalities. The site, along with Box Office Mojo and Withoutabox, is a subsidiary of Amazon.com, Inc.

National Public Radio

http://www.npr.org

Well-documented news and information, archived, often in audio or podcast form.

Open Secrets Center for Responsive Politics

https://www.opensecrets.org

The Center for Responsive Politics tracks financial contributions to political campaigns, individuals, and issues. The goal is to educate voters about the impact of money on elections and public policy.

PBS Learning Media

http://www.pbslearningmedia.org

Contains daily news, features, and information for students.

Pew Research Center

http://pewresearch.org

The Pew Research Center calls itself "a nonpartisan 'fact tank' that provides information on the issues, attitudes and trends shaping America and the world." Its reports and surveys are widely considered reliable, useful tools in helping a media critic better understand global attitudes and issues.

Source Watch

http://www.sourcewatch.org/index.php/SourceWatch

Because you want to be aware of detailed information that seems to be heavily biased in favor of a product, industry, or controversial individual, you can determine what organizations and potential biases are behind what advocacy groups and websites by checking the database at the Center for Media and Democracy's SourceWatch website.

Happy researching!

Appendix B: Media Ownership

What stories are told in mass media today? The answer to that question is determined by who gets to tell the story. This relates directly to our questions about media independence in this book. As we've seen, media independence is inextricable from its honesty—and its productivity.

Who gets to tell the story? What biases or controls might hinder independence? The control of our stories by large media corporations bothers many observant media critics, including the media diversity advocacy group Free Press. "Massive corporations dominate the U.S. media landscape," write Free Press advocates at the group's website. "Through a history of mergers and acquisitions, these companies have concentrated their control over what we see, hear and read."[1]

Media activists and reformers today work relentlessly on media reform issues that include providing universal and affordable Internet access and regulating corporate ownership of large media companies. In his book, *Rich Media, Poor Democracy*, media scholar Robert McChesney notes that people in the United States, and around the world, are less likely to be informed, participatory members of a democracy when media choices are controlled by fewer and fewer corporate media giants. "The media system has become increasingly concentrated and conglomerated into a relative handful of corporate hands," McChesney writes. "This concentration accentuates the core tendencies of a profit-driven, advertising-supported media system;

hypercommercialism and denigration of journalism and public service. It is a poison pill for democracy."[2]

Organizations like Free Press educate people and lobby lawmakers about the importance of media diversity—many voices in the great marketplace of ideas that is our media. Among the under-represented groups in media, Free Press contends, are women and people of color. Women are more than half of the U.S. population but hold fewer than 7 percent of all TV and radio station licenses; people of color are now more than one-third of the U.S. population but hold around 7 percent of radio licenses and 3 percent of TV licenses.[3]

To help you become aware of media concentration issues, I've listed below several of the largest U.S. media corporations, along with some of their subsidiaries or smaller properties owned by the larger corporations.

A detailed database of media ownership is available at the *Columbia Journalism Review*'s resource "Who Owns What" webpage: http://www.cjr.org/resources/. Free Press crafted an interactive media ownership chart "Who Owns the Media" here: http://www.freepress.net/ownership/chart.

Media companies listed on 2013 *Forbes* Fortune 500, as determined by size of sales, profits, assets, and market value.

(Note: *Forbes* lists only U.S. corporations. Not included on this list are large global media corporations like Bertelsmann AG, considered to be one of the world's largest media companies with dozens of broadcast and print media subsidiaries.)

Apple
(Revenue: $156.5 billion)

Although it's been best known as a company that makes media gizmos, Apple's content business is booming at iTunes' music and app store. Customers spent more than $10 billion on apps in 2013, making it the biggest year for app sales in history.[4]

General Electric
(Revenue: $146.9 billion)

The company, known for appliances and aircraft, has branched out into banking and insurance—and media. GE has sold its majority interest in its company NBC Universal to cable giant Comcast. However, GE still owns 49 percent of NBC Universal, including the NBC TV network, 24 TV stations, three movie companies, a handful of websites (including Fandango), and a few dozen cable networks—including Telemundo (16 stations), USA Network, SyFy, CNBC, MSNBC, Bravo, Oxygen, Chiller, E!, the Golf Channel, Sleuth, and Style.

AT&T
(Revenue: $127.4 billion)

The largest company providing phone service in the United States, AT&T also provides wireless and cable service to a huge swath of the nation. Since we get most of our information from the Internet these days on computers and mobile devices, the companies that control our access are worthy of note as media companies.

Verizon
(Revenue: $115.8 billion)

The second-largest phone company in the United States, Verizon has entered into a partnership with media giants like Comcast, Time Warner Cable, and Cox Communications so that each company will market and sell the others' services.[5]

Microsoft
(Revenue: $73.7 billion)

Microsoft produces the largest computer operating system in the world, Windows. It runs the No. 2 search engine, Bing, makes the XBox 360 gaming console, and owns Skype, the Internet-based audio and video conferencing software.

Comcast
(Revenue: $62.6 billion)

For starters, Comcast is the largest cable Internet, TV, and phone provider in the United States. It also owns a controlling interest in NBC Universal, some of the properties of which are listed above under General Electric. It owns about 80 properties within its Comcast Ventures division, including TiVo, About.com, blogging sites, and a bunch of e-commerce sites selling everything from used books to cars. A planned $45 billion merger with Time Warner Cable in 2014 would make Comcast a media behemoth. At the time of this writing, the merger had not yet been approved by the Federal Communications Commission.[6]

Amazon.com
(Revenue: $61.1 billion)

The company that started out selling books online in 1994 has become a gigantic online retailer of everything. Does this make Amazon a media company? The company's service, Amazon Prime, seems to be gaining traction as a new way of delivering media content to any device that can get streaming Internet. In 2013, company founder Jeff Bezos bought the family-owned Washington Post media company for $250 million. These days, Amazon's a media company to watch.

Google
(Revenue: $52.2 billion)

OK, it's the top search engine in the world—accordingly, it's also the top seller of online advertising in the world. Google's side gigs include the creation of the Android operating system, the top-selling operating system for mobile devices. Google owns YouTube and more than 30 other companies, including Adscape and DoubleClick—the latter tracks users' interests (what you've been searching for on Google) and delivers advertising that corresponds with that personal data.

The Walt Disney Company
(Revenue: $42.3 billion)

Disney isn't just another name for a Mickey Mouse cartoon or feature-length animations about the circle of life. The company's holdings are vast and global, and they include:

- 10 film and theater companies (Touchstone, Marvel, Pixar, etc.)

- 2 record labels

- 20-plus TV and cable stations

- ABC Television Network (ABC Daytime, ABC Entertainment, and ABC News)

- 80 percent of ESPN (with its 15 subsidiaries)

- 35 radio stations

- 10 publishing houses, plus ESPN's magazine and book publishing arms

- Disney resorts

- A cruise line

- Baby Einstein

- The Muppets Studio

- Club Penguin

- Disney Consumer Products (toys, T-shirts, food, stationery, footwear, etc.)

News Corporation
(Revenue: $33.7)

Another sprawler of a media corporation, though the company in 2013 spun off 21st Century Fox, its film division. Not to worry, stockholders. The new News Corp. still controlled the following:

- 20 cable stations (Fox News Channel, Fox Sports, FX, etc.)

- 27 TV stations

- A percentage of satellite TV services (BSkyB) that operate internationally

- 30 international television stations (in Asia, Africa, Europe, South America)

- Almost 30 U.S. newspapers including *The Wall Street Journal* and *New York Post*

- Dow Jones Averages

- Dow Jones Newswires

- Dow Jones Indexes

- 15 international newspapers including London's *The Times*

- Four magazines

- More than 40 book publishing imprints (Avon, HarperCollins, Zondervon, etc.)

- 17 online properties including AmericanIdol.com

Time Warner
(Revenue: $28.7 billion)

Owns:

- Home Box Office (HBO) with its 25 subsidiary companies, including Cinemax

- Turner Broadcasting System with dozens of subsidiaries, including the Cable News Network (CNN) and Cartoon Networks in every corner of the globe from Thailand to Sweden to Venezuela

- Time, Inc., with about 122 magazines (*Time, Entertainment Weekly, InStyle, Marie Claire, Money, People,* to name a few)

- Time Warner Investment Group (about 30 companies)

- DC Entertainment

- New Line Cinema

- Warner Bros. Pictures Group

- Warner Bros. Television Group

- Warner Bros. Home Entertainment Group

- Warner Bros. Consumer Products

Time Warner Cable
(Revenue: $21.4 billion)

The second-largest cable and Internet provider in the United States split from Time Warner in 2008. Cable giant Comcast offered $45 billion to buy Time Warner Cable, a deal that was pending FCC approval as of this writing. As a savvy media critic might observe, a merger like this would put most of the nation in the hands of one mega-cable company. Just a few years ago, such a deal would not have been possible, as a Federal Communications Commission rule stopped one cable company from owning more than 30 percent of the nation's total cable subscribers. In 2009, the U.S. Court of Appeals struck down the FCC's rule.

Viacom
(Revenue: $13.9 billion)

A company, National Amusements, owns controlling interests (71%) in Viacom and CBS, which spun off from Viacom in 2006. Both companies control plenty of media, and both are controlled by the owners of National Amusements. Who's that? Well, Sumner Redstone owns 80 percent of National Amusements, according to a report in the *Denver Post*, and Redstone's daughter Shari Redstone owns 20 percent.[7] Sumner Redstone is the chairman of Viacom and CBS.

Viacom's holdings include:

- More than 30 cable stations and networks (Comedy Central, MTV, VH1, BET, Spike, CMT, Nickelodeon, etc.)

- Film companies (including Paramount, MTV, Nickelodeon)

- Digital properties (including EPIX; iCarly.com; PetPetPark.com; SouthParkStudios.com)

McGraw Hill
(Revenue: $6.5 billion)

The McGraw Hill Companies has two branches. Its financial arm includes subsidiaries like Standard & Poors Ratings Services, a leading provider of credit ratings, Dow Jones Indices, J.D. Power, and McGraw Hill Construction. Its education arm is a leading publisher of textbooks and standardized tests, including the TerraNova Common Core tests.

Gannett
(Revenue: $5.4 billion)

Owns:

- Almost 100 newspapers around the United States, including *USA Today*

- A health care publication group with seven publications

- A government media group with 11 publications, one for each division of the U.S. military

- 15 newspapers in the United Kingdom

- 22 television stations

- 14 digital properties (MomsLikeMe.com; Career-Builder.com)

- 14 investment properties (Apartments.com; Cars.com; Homefinder.com)

- Eight other companies (Gannett Education, Gannett Regional Toning Centers)

Facebook
(Revenue: $5.1 billion)

Its ranking of No. 482 on the Forbes 500 list in 2013 marked a first for Facebook. The company, founded in 2004, has been a publicly traded corporation since 2012. Since the site is free for users, the site's revenue comes from various advertising sales and strategies and via its virtual gift shop.

As of September 2013, Facebook boasted:

- 1.19 billion monthly active users 874 million monthly active users who used Facebook mobile products

- 727 million daily active users on average, with about 80 percent outside the United States and Canada

Appendix C: 45 Intriguing Books

Bissell, Tom. *Extra Lives: Why Video Games Matter.* New York: Pantheon, 2010.

Botzakis, Stergios. *What's Your Source? Questioning the News.* New York: Fact Finders, 2008.

Clover, Carol. *Men, Women, and Chain Saws: Gender in the Modern Horror Film.* Princeton, N.J.: Princeton University Press, 1993.

De Zengotita, Thomas. *Mediated: How the Media Shapes Your World and The Way You Live In It.* New York: Bloomsbury, 2005.

Douglas, Susan. *Where the Girls Are: Growing Up Female with Mass Media.* New York: Three Rivers Press, 1995.

During, Simon. *The Cultural Studies Reader.* London: Routledge, 1993.

Fainaru-Wada, Mark, and Lance Williams. *Game of Shadows: Barry Bonds, BALCO, the Steroids Scandal That Rocked Professional Sports.* New York: Gotham, 2006.

Frank, Thomas. *The Conquest of Cool: Business Culture, Counterculture, and the Rise of Hip Consumerism.* Chicago: University of Chicago Press, 1998.

Gabler, Neil. *Life The Movie: How Entertainment Conquered Reality.* New York: Vintage Books, 1998.

Gigi, Durham, Meenakshi. *The Lolita Effect*. Woodstock, N.Y.: Overlook Press, 2008.

Gitlin, Todd. *Media Unlimited: How the Torrent of Images and Sounds Overwhelms Our Lives*. New York: Holt, 2002.

Glassner, Barry. *The Culture of Fear: Why Americans Are Afraid of the Wrong Things: Crime, Drugs, Minorities, Teen Moms, Killer Kids, Mutant Microbes, Plane Crashes, Road Rage, and So Much More*. New York: Basic Books, 1999.

Gonzalez, Juan, and Joseph Torres. *News for All The People: The Epic Story of Race and the American Media*. Brooklyn, N.Y.: Verso, 2011.

Grant, Barry Keith. *The Dread of Difference: Gender and the Horror Film*. Austin: University of Texas Press, 1996.

Graydon, Shari. *Made You Look: How Advertising Works and Why You Should Know*. Toronto: Annick Press, 2003.

Herman, Edward, and Noam Chomsky. *Manufacturing Consent: The Political Economy of the Mass Media*. 1988. Reprint, New York: Pantheon, 2002.

Holt, Jason. *The Daily Show and Philosophy: Moments of Zen in the Art of Fake News*. New York: Wiley-Blackwell, 2007.

Howe, Jeff. *Crowdsourcing: Why The Power of the Crowd Is Driving the Future of Business*. New York: Three Rivers, 2008.

Irwin, William, Mark T. Conrad, and Aeon J. Skoble, eds. *The Simpsons and Philosophy: The D'oh of Homer*. New York: Open Court, 2001.

Johnson, Clay A. *The Information Diet: A Case for Conscious Consumption*. Sebastapol, Calif.: O'Reilly, 2012.

Johnson, Marilyn. *This Book Is Overdue: How Librarians and Cybrarians Can Save Us All*. New York: Harper, 2010.

Johnson, Steven. *Everything Bad Is Good for You*. New York: Riverhead, 2006.

Keen, Andrew. *Digital Vertigo: How Today's Online Social Revolution Is Dividing, Diminishing, and Disorienting Us*. New York: St. Martin's Press, 2012.

Kilbourne, Jean. *Can't Buy My Love: How Advertising Changes The Way We Think and Feel*. New York: Free Press, 2000.

Klein, Naomi. *No Logo*. New York: Picador, 2002. First published Toronto: Knopf, Canada, 2000.

Kovach, Bill, and Tom Rosenstiel. *The Elements of Journalism: What Newspeople Should Know and What the Public Should Expect*. New York: Three Rivers, 2007.

Lanier, Jaron. *You Are Not a Gadget: A Manifesto*. New York: Vintage Books, 2010.

Lasn, Kalle. *Culture Jam: How to Reverse America's Suicidal Consumer Binge—And Why We Must*. New York: Harper-Collins, 1999.

Linn, Susan. *Consuming Kids: The Hostile Takeover of Childhood*. New York: New Press, 2004.

Lots, Amanda. *The Television Will Be Revolutionized*. New York: New York University Press, 2007.

McChesney, Robert W. *Rich Media, Poor Democracy: Communication Politics in Dubious Times*. Chicago: University of Illinois Press, 1999.

McLuhan, Marshall. *Understanding Media: The Extensions of Man*. Cambridge, Mass.: MIT Press, 1994. First published New York: McGraw-Hill, 1964.

Negroponte, Nicholas. *Being Digital*. New York: Vintage Books, 1995.

Orenstein, Peggy. *Cinderella Ate My Daughter: Dispatches From the Front Lines of the New Girlie-Girl Culture*. New York: Harper, 2011.

Pike, Deidre. *Enviro-Toons: Green Themes in Animated Cinema and Television*. Jefferson, N.C.: McFarland, 2012.

Postman, Neil. *Amusing Ourselves to Death: Public Discourse in the Age of Show Business*. New York: Penguin, 1985.

———. *How to Watch TV News*. New York: Penguin, 1992.

———. *Technopoly: The Surrender of Culture to Technology*. New York: Vintage Books, 2002.

Pozner, Jennifer L. *Reality Bites Back: The Troubling Truth About Guilty Pleasure TV*. Berkeley, Calif.: Seal, 2010.

Quart, Alissa. *Branded: The Buying and Selling of Teenagers*. New York: Perseus, 2003.

Rushkoff, Douglas. *Coercion: Why We Listen to What "They" Say*. New York: Riverhead, 1999.

———. *Media Virus: Hidden Agendas in Popular Culture*. New York: Ballantine Books, 1996.

Stark, Steven D. *Glued to the Set: The 60 Television Shows and Events That Made Us Who We Are Today*. New York: Delta, 1997.

Stratyner, Leslie, and James R. Keller, eds. *The Deep End of South Park: Critical Essays on TV's Shocking Cartoon Series.* Jefferson, N.C.: McFarland, 2009.

Zirin, Dave. *A People's History of Sports in the United States: 250 Years of Politics, Protest, People, and Play.* New York: New Press, 2008.

Notes

Introduction: Media Stories on Which We Feed

1. Quoted in Steven D. Stark, *Glued to the Set: The 60 Television Shows and Events That Made Us Who We Are Today* (New York: Delta, 1997), 49.

2. About 8,000 people showed up to audition in Detroit, Michigan, and more than 3,000 at other cities visited by the show's crew in 2013. Pat Healy, "*American Idol* Promises the Auditions are Coming." Metro.us, July 31, 2013. http://www.metro.us/newyork/entertainment/2013/07/31/american-idol-promises/.

3. Hannah Trierweiler Hudson, "Q&A With *Hunger Games* Author Suzanne Collins," Scholastic.com, http://www.scholastic.com/teachers/article/qa-hunger-games-author-suzanne-collins.

4. Ibid.

5. First Amendment to the U.S. Constitution: "Congress shall make no law respecting an establishment of religion, or prohibiting the free exercise thereof; or abridging the freedom of speech, or of the press; or the right of the people peaceably to assemble, and to petition the Government for a redress of grievances."

6. William Holmes McGuffey, *McGuffey's Second Eclectic Reader,* rev. ed. (New York: American Book, 1920), 126.

7. Number of those who watched one of the three commercial broadcast news programs on ABC, CBS, or NBC on an average night in 2011. From Emily Guskin, and Tom Rosenstiel, *The State of News Media 2012*, The Pew Research Center Project for Excellence in Journalism, no date, http://stateofthemedia.org/2012/network-news-the-pace-of-change-accelerates/.

8. Christmas was celebrated long before television, but shows like "A Charlie Brown Christmas" and "Frosty the Snowman"

have become tightly linked to our understanding of the holiday. On the other hand, Super Bowl Sunday did not exist before television. In fact, the cultural tradition of holding a party with plenty of chips and bubbly drinks to watch the Big Game only exists because mass media forces created this bit of culture.

9. One example of affecting personal lives: An individual who watches every episode of *How I Met Your Mother* might begin to believe that relationships are magical acts of fate, that certain couples are meant to be together. Do these ideas, driven into our collective psyche, make it harder to put time and effort into a relationship that seems less magical? That seems a question worthy of a media critic's research.

10. By the end of the class discussion, my students agreed that, yup, it does.

11. Douglas Rushkoff, *Coercion: Why We Listen to What "They" Say* (New York: Riverhead, 1999), 24.

12. Ibid.

13. Naomi Klein spoke at Humboldt State University in Arcata, Calif., on December 6, 2013. Her book, *This Changes Everything: Capitalism Versus the Climate,* was published by Simon & Schuster in 2014.

14. Rushkoff, 25.

Chapter 1: Care and Feeding of Mediated Me

1. Quoted in "Essay: The Playboy Interview Marshall McLuhan," *Playboy*, March 1969. Reprinted at Next Nature. net, http://www.nextnature.net/2009/12/the-playboy -interview-marshall-mcluhan/.

2. *How Much Information? A 2009 Report on American Consumers* (San Diego: Global Information Industry Center, University of California, San Diego, January 2010), http://hmi.ucsd.edu/ howmuchinfo_research_report_consum.php.

3. Time spent doing two things at once was counted twice. An hour watching TV and surfing the Net is two hours of info interaction.

4. *How Much Information?*

5. David Buckingham, *Media Education: Literacy, Learning and Contemporary Culture* (Malden, Mass.: Polity, 2003), 28

6. Ibid., 27.

7. Walter Lippmann, *Public Opinion* (1922; repr., New York: Free Press, 1997), 10.

8. "Media," Dictionary.com, http://dictionary.reference.com/browse/media.

9. Lippmann, 11.

10. Bill Kovach and Tom Rosenstiel, *The Elements of Journalism: What Newspeople Should Know and the Public Should* Expect (New York: Three Rivers Press, 2007), 2, 5.

11. Ibid., 5.

12. Victor Navasky, "Profiles in Cowardice," *The Nation,* November 5, 2001, http://www.thenation.com/issue/november-5-2001.

13. The largest media corporations are Time-Warner, which owns a long list of magazines, film companies, cable TV networks; Comcast, a cable provider with a controlling interest in the NBC Universal network of TV stations and movie companies, among other entities; News Corporation, which owns newspapers, the Fox TV network, magazines, etc.; Viacom (cable networks and movie companies) is controlled as is CBS's TV stations and publishing division by National Amusements; The Walt Disney Company owns movie studios, theme parks, magazines, and more. See Appendix B on media ownership.

14. Marshall McLuhan, *Understanding Media: The Extensions of Man* (1964; repr. Cambridge, Mass.: MIT Press, 1994), 311.

15. Edward S. Herman and Noam Chomsky, *Manufacturing Consent: The Political Economy of Mass Media.* (1988; repr. New York: Pantheon, 2002), 14.

16. Quoted in Liam Fahey and Robert M. Randall, *Learning from the Future: Competitive Foresight Scenarios* (New York: John Wiley & Sons, 1998), 332.

17. W. James Potter, *Media Literacy*, 5th ed. (Los Angeles: Sage, 2011), 249.

18. Nineteenth-century novelist Horatio Alger wrote about 100 books for young men, lauding the rewards of a virtuous life. In Alger's fictions, any young man could achieve the American Dream through hard work and clean living no matter how humble his original circumstances might be.

19. George Gerbner, "Reclaiming our Cultural Mythology: Television's Global Marketing Strategy Creates a Damaging and Alienated Window on the World." *The Ecology of Justice* (Spring 1994): 40.

20. Ibid.

21. Ibid.

Chapter 2: Print Media

1. HarperCollins is owned by News Corporation. *The Oprah Winfrey Show* was a CBS Corp. product, part of Viacom CEO's Sumner Redstone's vast media empire.

2. "A Million Little Lies: Exposing James Frey's Fiction Addiction," The Smoking Gun, January 4, 2006, http://www.thesmokinggun.com/documents/celebrity/million-little-lies.

3. David Carr, "How Oprah Trumped Truthiness," *New York Times,* January 30, 2006, http://www.nytimes.com/2006/01/30/business/media/30carr.html.

4. "Field Listing: Literacy," *CIA World Factbook,* https://www.cia.gov/library/publications/the-world-factbook/fields/2103.html.

5. Kathryn Zickuhr and Lee Rainey, "Snapshot of Reading in America in 2013," Pew Research Internet Project, January 16, 2014, http://www.pewinternet.org/2014/01/16/a-snapshot-of-reading-in-america-in-2013/.

6. "Reading on the Rise: A New Chapter in American Literacy," National Endowment for the Arts, 2009, http://arts.gov/sites/default/files/ReadingonRise.pdf.

7. In an August 1896, column headlined, "Business Announcement," *New York Times* publisher Adolph Ochs wrote of the "sincere desire to conduct a high-standard newspaper, clean, dignified, and trustworthy," which would require "honesty, watchfulness, earnestness, industry and practical knowledge applied with common sense."

8. Lori Robertson, "Shattered Glass at *The New Republic*: How Fabricating Author Stephen Glass Was Brought Down," *American Journalism Review* (June 1998), http://www.ajr.org/article.asp?id=1838.

9. Bill Kovach and Tom Rosenstiel. *The Elements of Journalism: What Newspeople Should Know and the Public Should Expect* (New York: Three Rivers Press, 2007), 90.

10. Franklin Foer, "The Source of the Trouble," *New York Magazine*, May 21, 2005, http://nymag.com/nymetro/news/media/features/9226/.

11. "News War," *PBS Frontline*, February 13, 2007, http://www.pbs.org/wgbh/pages/frontline/newswar/.

12. "The Times and Iraq," *New York Times*, May 26, 2004, http://www.nytimes.com/2004/05/26/international/middleeast/26FTE_NOTE.html.

13. Lizette Alvarez, "A Florida Law Gets Scrutiny after a Teenager's Killing," *New York Times*, March 20, 2012; updated April 5, 2012, http://www.nytimes.com/2012/03/21/us/justice-department-opens-inquiry-in-killing-of-trayvon-martin.html#.

14. "Jim Lehrer with Ben Bradlee," *PBS Newshour*, June 19, 2006, http://www.pbs.org/newshour/bradlee/transcript_ethics.html.

15. Kovach and Rosenstiel, 118.

16. Ibid., 115.

17. "Colorado Springs Independent," Association of Alternative Newsmedia, no date, http://www.altweeklies.com/aan/colorado-springs-independent/Company?oid=17.

18. "About AAN," Association of Alternative Newsmedia, no date, http://www.altweeklies.com/aan/about-aan/Page.

19. Tinker V. Des Moines School Dist., 393 U.S. 503." Decided February. 24, 1969. http://supcourt.ntis.gov/get_case. html?casename=Case Name: TINKER V. DES MOINES SCHOOL DIST., 393 U.S. 503 &searchstring=mode=casename&cn_ words1=tinker&cn_words2=des moines.

20. "The Student Press Law Center's High School Top 10 List," Student Press Law Center, http://www.splc.org/ knowyourrights/legalresearch.asp?id=3.

21. Emily Summars, "Editor Files Grievance After Ill. School Censors Pro-Discipline Editorial," Student Press Law Center, March 9, 2012, http://www.splc.org/news/newsflash. asp?id=2346.

22. Joshua Benton, "Clay Shirky: Let a Thousand Flowers Bloom to Replace Newspapers," Nieman Journalism Lab, September 23, 2009, http://www.niemanlab.org/2009/09/ clay-shirky-let-a-thousand-flowers-bloom-to-replace-newspapers-dont-build-a-paywall-around-a-public-good/.

23. "20 Stories That Made A Difference: For Better or Worse," Fairness and Accuracy in Reporting, January–February 2006, http://www.fair.org/index.php?page=2816.

24. "Meet the Exonerated," Northwestern Law, Center on Wrongful Convictions, no date, http://www.law.northwestern. edu/cwc/exonerations/ilWilliamsDSummary.html.

25. Erica Smith, "Paper Cuts," Newspaperlayoffs.com, 2012, http://newspaperlayoffs.com.

26. Danny Sullivan, "Google CEO Eric Schmidt on Newspapers and Journalism," Search Engine Land, October 2, 2009, http://searchengineland.com/ google-ceo-eric-schmidt-on-newspapers-journalism-27172.

Chapter 3: Parody News

1. "To Kill a Mockingturd," The Daily Show with Jon Stewart website, aired May 2, 2011, http://www.thedailyshow.com/ watch/mon-may-2-2011/to-kill-a-mockingturd.

2. One example: "Great Moments in Punditry—The O'Reilly Factor," The Daily Show with Jon Stewart website, aired June 14, 2005, http://www.thedailyshow.com/watch/tue-june-14-2005/great-moments-in-punditry---the-o-reilly-factor.

3. "Americans Spend More Time Following the News," The Pew Research Center for People & the Press, September 12, 2010, http://www.people-press.org/2010/09/12/americans-spending-more-time-following-the-news/.

4. "Today's Journalists Less Prominent," The Pew Research Center for People & the Press, press release, March 8, 2007, 6. http://www.people-press.org/files/legacy-pdf/309.pdf.

5. Rachel Sotos, "The Fake News as the Fifth Estate," in *The Daily Show and Philosophy*, ed. Jason Holt, 33 (Malden, MA: Blackwell, 2007).

6. "The George Orwell Award," National Council of Teachers of English, http://www.ncte.org/volunteer/groups/publiclangcom/orwellaward.

7. "Bad New Baier," The Daily Show with Jon Stewart website, aired March 31, 2011, http://www.thedailyshow.com/watch/thu-march-31-2011/bad-news-baier.

8. "Exclusive: Jon Stewart on Fox News Suday," Fox News website, aired June 19, 2011, http://video.foxnews.com/v/1007046245001/exclusive-jon-stewart-on-fox-news-sunday/.

9. "Viacom Vs. Google," The Daily Show with Jon Stewart website, aired March 22, 2007. http://www.thedailyshow.com/watch/thu-march-22-2007/viacom-vs--youtube.

10. Stewart's annual income from all sources was $14 million in 2009, *Forbes* reported. "The Celebrity 100: #83 Jon Stewart," Forbes.com, June 3, 2009, http://www.forbes.com/lists/2009/53/celebrity-09_Jon-Stewart_JZY4.html.

11. "Daily Show Viewers Ace Political Quiz," CNN.com, September 29, 2004, http://www.cnn.com/2004/SHOWBIZ/TV/09/28/comedy.politics/index.html.

12. "Public Knowledge of Current Affairs Little Changed by News and Information Revolutions: What Americans Know: 1989–2007," Pew Research Center for People & the Press,

April 15, 2007, http://www.people-press.org/2007/04/15/
public-knowledge-of-current-affairs-little-changed-by-news-
and-information-revolutions/.

13. "Barack Obama Gives Daily Show Biggest Ever Audience,"
The Guardian, October 31, 2008, http://www.guardian.co.uk/
media/2008/oct/31/ustelevision-barackobama.

14. "Rally to Restore Sanity and/or Fear," Comedy Central
website, http://www.comedycentral.com/shows/rally_to_
restore_sanity_and_or_fear /index.jhtml.

15. "Immigrant Farm Workers," C-Span Video Library, September 24, 2010, http://www.c-spanvideo.org/program
/295639-1.

16. Sotos, 38.

Chapter 4: Social Networks

1. Mark Leiren-Young, *The Green Chain: Nothing Is Ever Clear
Cut* (New York: Heritage House, 2010), 100.

2. "Ben Rattrey," The Daily Show with Jon Stewart website,
aired April 23, 2012, http://www.thedailyshow.com/watch/
mon-april-23-2012/ben-rattray.

3. Malcolm Gladwell, "Small Change: Why the Revolution
Will Not Be Tweeted," *The New Yorker*, October 4, 2010, http://
www.newyorker.com/reporting/2010/10/04/101004fa_fact
_gladwell.

4. Cristina Corbin, "Pro-Kremlin Viral Video Portrays Ukraine
Invading Russia." Fox News. April 9, 2014. http://www.
foxnews.com/world/2014/04/09/pro-kremlin-viral-video-seeks-
to-portray-fictious-tale-war-with-ukraine/.

5. Eric Louw, "Social Media = Revolution?" The Vision
Machine, April 9, 2013, http://thevisionmachine.com/2013
/04/facebook-revolutions/.

6. Jeff Bercovici, "First Facebook Killed MySpace. Now It's Sav-
ing It," *Forbes*, February 13, 2012, http://www.forbes.com
/sites/jeffbercovici/2012/02/13/first-facebook-killed-myspace
-now-its-saving-it/.

7. MySpace was sold for $35 million in 2011 and is reemerging as a music player network, competing with Pandora and Rhapsody.

8. "Newsroom Fact Sheet," Facebook, http://newsroom.fb.com/content/default.aspx?NewsAreaId=22.

9. If it were a nation, Facebook's population ranks it third in the world—below China and India with considerably more than twice as many "citizens" as the United States.

10. Bianca Bosker, "Twitter Finally Shares Key Stats: 40 Percent of Active Users Are Lurkers," *Huffington Post,* September 8, 2011, http://www.huffingtonpost.com/2011/09/08/twitter-stats_n_954121.html.

11. "Internet Gains on Television as Public's Main News Source," Pew Research Center for People & the Press, January 4, 2011, http://www.people-press.org/2011/01/04/internet-gains-on-television-as-publics-main-news-source/.

12. Ki Mae Huessner, "7 Twitter Hoaxes and Half-Truths," ABC News, January 15, 2010, http://abcnews.go.com/Technology/twitter-hoaxes-half-truths/story?id=9565678#.T5rUSb9x6BS.

13. "Twitter Guide Book: How to, Tips and Instructions by Mashable," Mashable.com, http://mashable.com/guidebook/twitter/.

14. "Internet Censorship in China," *New York Times,* March 22, 2010, http://topics.nytimes.com/topics/news/international/countriesandterritories/china/internet_censorship/index.html.

15. Quoted in Ali Bell, "China's Closed Magic Window—Google.cn," *New Media Gazette,* AUT University, https://www.newmediajournalism.aut.ac.nz/archive/2006/ass04/yxn1020_ass04.html.

16. Sylvia Hui, "Google, Microsoft Block Child Abuse Search Results," ABCnews.go.com, November 18, 2013, http://abcnews.go.com/Technology/wireStory/google-searches-child-abuse-sites-blocked-20921368.

17. Adrian Chen, "Inside Facebook's Outsourced Anti-Porn and Gore Brigade, Where 'Camel Toes' Are More Offensive

Than 'Crushed Heads,'" Gawker.com, February 16, 2012, http://gawker.com/5885714/.

18. "Community Standards," Facebook, November 18, 2013, https://www.facebook.com/communitystandards.

19. Lee Rowland, "Naked Statue Reveals One Thing: Facebook Censorship Needs Better Appeals Process," ACLU.org, September 25, 2013, https://www.aclu.org/blog/technology-and-liberty-national-security/naked-statue-reveals-one-thing-facebook-censorship.

20. Abby Ohlheiser, "Shareholders Balk at Citigroup CEO's Pay Package," *Slate* April 18, 2012, http://slatest.slate.com/posts/2012/04/18/vikram_s_pandit_ceo_pay_package_gets_no_vote_from_citigroup_shareholders.html.

Chapter 5: Advertising

1. James B. Twitchell, *Adcult USA: The Triumph of Advertising in American Culture* (New York: Columbia University Press, 1996), 4.

2. Michael D'Estries, "Bud Light Super Bowl Ads Plugs Rescue Dogs," Mother Nature Network, http://www.mnn.com/family/pets/blogs/bud-light-super-bowl-ad-plugs-rescue-dogs.

3. "2012 Super Bowl Ads That Nailed Customer Engagement," Super Bowl Ads, February 17, 2012, http://superbowl-ads.com/article_archive/2012/02/17/2012-super-bowl-ads-that-nailed-customer-engagement/.

4. "8. Flawsome." *12 Trends for 2012.* Trendwatching.com, http://trendwatching.com/trends/12trends2012/?flawsome.

5. A website lures young people in by suggesting that companies are willing to "lease your forehead for $5,000" if the person agrees to wear temporary commercial tattoos for several years. At Lease Your Body (http://www.leaseyourbody.com), a forehead tattoo appears to be going for about $1,000

6. Lousie Story, "Anywhere the Eye Can See, It's Likely to See an Ad," *New York Times,* January 15, 2007, http://www.nytimes.com/2007/01/15/business/media/15everywhere.html.

7. Quoted in "Forum: So How Should We Think About All of This?" *The Persuaders*. PBS.org. November 9, 2004, http://www. pbs.org/wgbh/pages/frontline/shows/persuaders/forum/.

8. "8. Flawsome."

9. James B. Twitchell, *AdCult USA: The Triumph of Advertising in U.S. Culture* (New York: Columbia University Press, 1996), 116–119.

10. Ibid.

11. Ibid., 117.

12. Philip H. Dougherty, "Cigarette Maker Cuts Off Agency That Made Smoking-Ban TV Ads," *New York Times* April 6, 1988, http://www.nytimes.com/1988/04/06/business/cigarette-maker-cuts-off-agency-that-made-smoking-ban-tv-ads.html.

13. Twitchell, 117.

14. Ross Hammond, "Tobacco Advertising & Promotion: The Need for a Coordinated Global Response" (paper presented at WHO International Conference on Global Tobacco Control Law: Towards a WHO Framework Convention on Tobacco Control, New Delhi, India, January 7–9, 2000), www.who.int/tobacco/media/ROSS2000X.pdf.

15. Ibid.

16. "Advertising to Children," Children Now, http://www.childrennow.org/index.php/learn/advertising_to_children.

17. David H. Jernigan and Craig Ross. "Monitoring Youth Exposure to Advertising on Television: The Devil Is in the Details," *Journal of Public Affairs* 10 (February–May 2010): 36–49.

18. Ibid.

19. Susan M. Liss, "CDC's Anti-Smoking Ad Campaign Spurred Over 100,000 Smokers to Quit; Media Campaigns Must be Expanded Nationally and in the States," Campaign for Tobacco-Free Kids, press release, September 9, 2013, http://www.tobaccofreekids.org/press_releases/post/2013_09_09_cdc.

20. Ed Gillespie, "Advertising in Itself Is Not Evil; It Is Just Communication," Guardian Sustainable Business blog, *The*

Guardian, November 3, 2011, http://www.theguardian.com/
sustainable-business/blog/advertising-sustainable
-communication-brand-marketing.

21. Ibid.

Chapter 6: Public Relations

1. "John Stauber: Author, Founder of PR Watch," first posted at
www.guerillanewsnetwork.com, a site that shut down in 2009.
Video now on Youtube.com.

2. Quoted in Dennis L. Wilcox and Glen T. Cameron, *Public
Relations: Strategies and Tactics,* 9th ed. (Boston: Allyn & Bacon,
2010), 41.

3. Hughes, Sarah Ann, "Kim Kardashian May Press Charges
on Flour Bomber After All," Celebritology 2.0, The Washington Post, March 26, 2012, http://www.washingtonpost.com/
blogs/celebritology/post/kim-kardashian-may-press-charges-
on-flour-bomber-after-all/2012/03/26/gIQAVF8mbS_blog.
html.

4. Kevin Bogardus, "PR Firm Took $1.2M from Gadhafi's
Libya," TheHill.com, July 18, 2011, http://thehill.com/business-
a-lobbying/172077-pr-firm-took-12m-from-gadhafis-libya.

5. Sheldon Rampton and John Stauber, *Trust Us, We're Experts:
How Industry Manipulates Science and Gambles with Your Future*
(New York: Most Tarcher/Putnam, 2002), 22–23.

6. "About Us," The Center for Media and Democracy's PR
Watch, http://www.prwatch.org/cmd.

7. Sabrina Siddiqui, "Restore Our Future, Romney SuperPac,
Runs Ads in Obama-Leaning Minnesota, New Mexico," *Huffington Post,* October 31, 2012, http://www.huffingtonpost.
com/2012/10/31/restore-our-future-ads-minnesota-new-
mexico_n_2049585.html.

8. Glen T. Cameron, Dennis L. Wilcox, Bryan H. Reber, and
Jae-Hwa Shin, *Public Relations Today: Managing Competition and
Conflict* (Boston: Pearson, 2008), 68.

9. "Public Affairs Campaign of the Year 2007: Porter Novelli
and Abundant Forests Alliance: Renew. Reuse. Respect," *PR*

Week March 8, 2007, http://www.prweek.com/article/1258616/
public-affairs-campaign-year-2007.

10. Wilcox and Cameron, 35.

11. "Public Affairs Campaign of the Year 2007: Porter Novelli
and Abundant Forests Alliance: Renew. Reuse. Respect."

12. Wilcox Cameron, 34.

13. "Land and Resources Management," U.S. Forest Service,
http://www.fs.usda.gov/land/dixie/landmanagement.

14. "Forest Resources of the United States," *National Atlas of the
United States,* U.S. Dept. of Interior, January 14, 2013, http://
nationalatlas.gov/articles/biology/a_forest.html.

15. "Abundant Forest Alliance," Sourcewatch, The Center for
Media and Democracy, April 13, 2008, http://sourcewatch.
org/index.php?title=Abundant_Forests_Alliance.

16. The Environmental Protection Agency defines a Superfund
site as is an uncontrolled or abandoned place where hazard-
ous waste is located, possibly affecting local ecosystems or
people.

17. Region 5 Superfund, St. Regis Paper Co. EPA.gov, January 2014, http://www.epa.gov/R5Super/npl/minnesota/
MND057597940.html.

18. David McAfee, "NCR, Int'l Paper Liable for Mill Superfund
Cleanup," Law360.com, September 26, 2013, http://www.
law360.com/articles/476154/ncr-int-l-paper-liable-for-mill
-superfund-cleanup.

19. Region 2 Superfund, Curtis Specialty Papers, EPA.gov,
July 23, 2014, http://www.epa.gov/region2/superfund/npl/
curtisspecialtypapers/.

20. Scott Leamon, "EPA Looks to Settle with MeadWestvaco on
Kim-Stan Landfill Clean-Up," WSLS-TV, September 16, 2013,
http://www.wsls.com/story/20817538/epa-looks-to-settle-with-
meadwestvaco-on-kim-stan-landfill-clean-up.

21. Clive Thompson, "The See-Through CEO," *Wired,* March
2007, http://www.wired.com/wired/archive/15.04/wired40_
ceo.html.

22. Terri Birkett, *Truax* (Chesterfield, Missouri: The National Wood Flooring Association, 1995), 12. http://woodfloors.org/truax.pdf.

23. Ibid., 10.

24. Lauren Daniels, "Lou Dobbs: Seuss's 'Lorax' Is Indoctrinating Kids," *Time.com*, February 23, 2012, http://newsfeed.time.com/2012/02/23/lou-dobbs-the-lorax-is-indoctrinating-american-children/.

25. Jeff Bercovici, "Dr. Seuss' Widow Says 'The Lorax' Is Education, Not Propaganda," *Forbes*, March 2, 2012, http://www.forbes.com/sites/jeffbercovici/2012/03/02/dr-seusss-widow-says-the-lorax-is-education-not-propaganda/.

26. Arif Durrani, "BP in £60m Advertising Blitz Following Oil Spill," BrandRepublic, September 2, 2012, http://www.brandrepublic.com/news/1025838/BP-60m-advertising-blitz-following-oil-spill/.

27. Durrani.

28. Dennis Dijkzeul and Markus Moke, "Public Communications Strategies of International Humanitarian Organizations," *International Review of the Red Cross* 87, no. 860 (December 2005), http://www.icrc.org/eng/assets/files/other/irrc_860_dijkzeul.pdf.

Chapter 7: Reality TV

1. Quoted in Dennis Lim, "Reality TV Originals, In Drama's Lens," *New York Times*, April 15, 2011, http://www.nytimes.com/2011/04/17/arts/television/hbos-cinema-verite-looks-at-american-family.html?scp=2&sq=an%20american%20family&st=cse.

2. Todd Gitlin, *Media Unlimited: How the Torrent of Images and Sounds Overwhelms Our Lives* (New York: Holt, 2002), 147.

3. Steven Reiss and James Wiltz, "Why America Loves Reality TV," *Psychology Today*, September 1, 2001; updated December 14, 2010, http://www.psychologytoday.com/articles/200109/why-america-loves-reality-tv.

4. David Bauder, "'American Idol' Ratings Down," *Huffington Post*, April 20, 2013, http://www.huffingtonpost.com/2013/04/30/american-idol-ratings-beaten-by-the-voice-dwts_n_3189265.html.

5. "About the Show," *American Idol* website, http://www.americanidol.com/about/.

6. Valerie Strauss, "SAT Question on Reality TV Stirs Controversy," *Washington Post*, March 15, 2011, http://www.washingtonpost.com/blogs/answer-sheet/post/sat-question-on-reality-tv-stirs-controversy/2011/03/15/ABjNyCY_blog.html.

7. Neil Postman, *Amusing Ourselves to Death: Public Discourse in the Age of Show Business* (1986; repr. New York: Penguin, 2006), 4.

8. Steven Stark, *Glued to the Set: The 60 Television Shows and Events That Made Us Who We Are Today* (New York: Delta, 1997), 99.

9. Quoted in "The Aftermath of the Quiz Show Scandal," *American Experience*, PBS website, http://www.pbs.org/wgbh/amex/quizshow/peopleevents/pande07.html.

10. Stark, 108.

11. Edward Wyatt, "TV Contestants: Tired, Tipsy and Pushed to Brink," *New York Times*, August 2, 2009, http://www.nytimes.com/2009/08/02/business/media/02reality.

12. Associated Press/TV Guide Study, IPSOS-Public Affairs, press release, September 9, 2005, 1, http://surveys.ap.org/data/Ipsos/national/2005/2005-09-08%20TV%20GUIDE%20Topline%20results.pdf.

13. Stark, 108.

14. Jill Weinberger and Joseph O'Dell, "Primetime Shows with Most Product Placement 2011," CNBC website, January 5, 2012, http://www.cnbc.com/id/45884892/Primetime_Shows_With_the_Most_Product_Placement?slide=1.

15. Jill Weinberger, and Joseph O'Dell, "Here Are 10 Primetime Shows with the Most Product Placement," Business Insider, January 7, 2012, http://mobile.businessinsider.com/these-10-primetime-tv-shows-most-product-placement-2012-1/1-american-idol-10.

16. A "guidette" is the female version of the guido, a guy from New York or New Jersey who works on his muscles, sports designer clothes, and wears plenty of jewelry. The guidette also dresses in tight clothes, wears cosmetics indulgently, and tends to "hook up" with some frequency.

17. James W. Potter, *Media Literacy* (Thousand Oaks, Calif.: Sage, 2011), 232.

18. Ibid., 237.

Chapter 8: Video Games

1. Mike Snider, "Are Video Games Art? Draw Your Own Conclusions," *USA Today,* March 12, 2012, http://www.usatoday.com/life/lifestyle/story/2012-03-12/video-games-smithsonian/53502696/1.

2. Ben Fritz, "Video Game Borrows Page from Hollywood Playbook," *Los Angeles Times,* November 18, 2009, http://articles.latimes.com/2009/nov/18/business/fi-ct-duty18.

3. Noel Gill, "10 Most Popular Facebook Games in 2012," Socialdon.com, April 5, 2012, http://www.socialdon.com/blog/popular-facebook-games-2012/.

4. Jefferson Graham, "How Often Do You Play Candy Crush Saga?" Talking Tech, *USA Today,* December 30, 2013, http://www.usatoday.com/story/tech/columnist/talkingtech/2013/12/30/candy-crush---how-many-times-did-you-play-it-in-2013/4246655/.

5. Reuters, "Factbox: A Look at the $65 Billion Video Games Industry," Reuters.com, June 6, 2011, http://uk.reuters.com/article/2011/06/06/us-videogames-factbox-idUKTRE7555 2I20110606.

6. Fritz.

7. Craig Anderson, "Violent Video Games: Myths, Facts, and Unanswered Questions," American Psychological Association, October 2003. http://www.apa.org/science/about/psa/2003/10/anderson.aspx.

8. James Newman, *Videogames* (New York: Routledge, 2004), 65.

9. Ibid., 61.

10. G. Frasca, quoted inn James Newman, *Videogames* (New York: Routledge, 2004), 27.

11. Rich Adams, Colossal Cave Adventure Page, http://www.rickadams.org/adventure/.

12. Entertainment Software Association, 2009, quoted in Stanley J. Baran, "Video Games," in *Media Literacy and Culture* (New York: McGraw-Hill, 2012), 245.

13. Caleb Scarf, "'Mass Effect' Solves the Fermi Paradox?" *Scientific American* Life, Unbounded blog, March 15, 2012. http://blogs.scientificamerican.com/life-unbounded/2012/03/15/mass-effect-solves-the-fermi-paradox/.

14. Ibid.

15. Stephen Totilo, "*Infamous 2* Is the Post-Katrina Video Game That America Deserves," Kotaku, July 18, 2011, http://kotaku.com/5822042/infamous-2-is-the-post+katrina-video-game-that-america-deserves.

16. Evan Narcisse, "The Goriest Video Game Deaths You'll See All Year, in Less Than a Minute," Kotaku, April 23, 2012, http://kotaku.com/5904269/the-most-detailed-video-game-deaths-youll-see-all-year-in-less-than-a-minute.

17. U.S. Army, "America's Army," http://www.americasarmy.com/aa/.

18. By 2009, U.S. taxpayers had spent about $33 million on the government's game, investing another $3 million a year or so in ongoing development. That sounds like a lot, especially to someone making minimum wage at the local hamburger joint. Actually, the number pales in comparison with, say, the projected $215 billion requested in 2012 to maintain and modernize the U.S. military's nuclear weapons stockpile for 10 years. In 2012, the U.S. Department of Defense spent $31 billion a year to keep its nukes in working order. If the U.S. budget were a pie, the portion devoted to video game development would be a tiny crumb.

19. American Civil Liberties Union, "Soldiers of Misfortune: Abusive U.S. Military Recruitment and Failure to Protect Child

Soldiers," May 13, 2008, http://www.aclu.org/human-rights/
soldiers-misfortune-abusive-us-military-recruitment-and-
failure-protect-child-soldiers.

20. Michael B. Reagan, "U.S. Military Recruits Children,"
Truthout.org, July 23, 2008, http://archive.truthout.org/article/
us-military-recruits-children.

21. Wee Ling Wong, Cuihua Shen, Luciano Nocera, et al.,
"Serious Video Game Effectiveness,"academia.edu, University of Southern California, Viterbi School of Engineering and
Annenberg School for Communication, 2007, http://galactus.
upf.edu/trac/bodylearning/raw.../p49-wong.pdf.

22. "Taiwan Teen Dies after Gaming for 40 Hours," *Australian
News,* August 2, 2012, http://www.theaustralian.com.au/news/
breaking-news/taiwan-teen-dies-after-gaming-for-40-hours/
story-fn3dxix6-1226428437223.

23. Darcia Narvaez, "Playing Violent Video Games: Good
or Bad?" *Psychology Today,* November 9, 2012, http://www.
psychologytoday.com/blog/moral-landscapes/201011/
playing-violent-video-games-good-or-bad.

24. David G. Savage, "Supreme Court Strikes Down California Video Game Law," *Los Angeles Times,* June 28,
2011, http://articles.latimes.com/2011/jun/28/nation/
la-na-0628-court-violent-video-20110628.

Chapter 9: Recorded Music and Celebrity Musicians

1. Neil Gaiman, *Anansi Boys* (London: Hodder Headline, 2005), 4.

2. Karen Bliss, "Does Michael Franti Agree with Neil Young,
That Music No Longer Has Power to Change the World?"
Samaritan Magazine, December 8, 2010. http://www.
samaritanmag.com/does-michael-franti-agree-neil-young-
music-no-longer-has-power-change-world.

3. Ibid.

4. "RIAA Tallies the Decade's Top Gold & Platinum Award
Winners," *Gold and Platinum News,* RIAA.com, February 7,
2010, http://riaa.com/newsitem.php?content_selector=riaa
-news-gold-and-platinum&news.

5. "Choice Quotes from the Justin Bieber Cover Story," *Rolling Stone,* 2012, http://www.rollingstone.com/music/pictures/the-tao-of-justin-bieber-20110216/0948229.

6. Ira Kalb, "Miley Cyrus and Justin Bieber Are Both Marketing Geniuses," *Business Insider,* October 17, 2013, http://www.businessinsider.com/cute-to-edgy-rebranding-lessons-from-miley-cyrus-and-justin-bieber-2013-10.

7. A dance move characterized by rapid hip thrusting in a semi-squatting stance.

8. Miley Cyrus, "Wrecking Ball," RCA Records, MileyCyrusVevo YouTube Channel, September 9, 2013, http://www.youtube.com/watch?v=My2FRPA3Gf8.

9. Kalb.

10. "Dixie Chicks Pulled from Air After Bashing Bush," CNN.com, March 14, 2003, http://www.cnn.com/2003/SHOWBIZ/Music/03/14/dixie.chicks.reut/.

11. Tom Waits, "Day After Tomorrow," Dailyshow.com, November 28, 2006, http://www.thedailyshow.com/watch/tue-november-28-2006/moment-of-zen---day-after-tomorrow.

12. Eminem, "Mosh," Interscope Geffen AM, 2004, InterscopeGeffenAM YouTube Channel, June 15, 2009, http://www.youtube.com/watch?v=Ox0Q4YIdnGI.

13. Markos Moulitsas, "The Politics of Mosh," *Daily Kos,* October 26, 2004, http://www.dailykos.com/story/2004/10/27/65089/-the-politics-of-Mosh#.

14. Bob Dylan, "Absolutely Sweet Marie," *Blonde on Blonde,* Columbia Records, 1966.

15. Seth Stevenson, "Tangled Up in Boobs: What's Bob Dylan Doing in a Victoria's Secret Ad?" *Slate,* April 12, 2004, http://www.slate.com/articles/business/ad_report_card/2004/04/tangled_up_in_boobs.html.

16. Charles R. Cross, *Heavier Than Heaven: A Biography of Kurt Cobain* (New York: Hyperion, 2001), 257.

17. "Nirvana Lithium MTV Awards," YouTube, February 17, 2011, http://www.youtube.com/watch?v=RIQ4tkfysn8&feature=related.

18. "Store Wars: When Wal-Mart Comes to Town," PBS.org, http://www.pbs.org/itvs/storewars/stores3.html.

19. "Ani DiFranco," Biography.com, A&E Networks, 2012, http://www.biography.com/people/ani-difranco-20874409.

20. Will Hermes, review of *Which Side Are You On?* by Ani DiFranco, *Rolling Stone*, January 17, 2012, http://www.rollingstone.com/music/albumreviews/which-side-are-you-on-20120117.

21. One man died of and the other was critically injured by self-inflicted gunshot wounds. They'd been drinking beer, smoking marijuana, and listening to Judas Priest music.

22. Marilyn Manson, "Columbine: Who's Fault Is It?" *Rolling Stone,* June 24, 1999, http://www.rollingstone.com/culture/news/columbine-whose-fault-is-it-19990624.

23. Michael Linton, "The Mozart Effect," *First Things* Issue Archive, March 1999, http://www.firstthings.com/article/2009/02/002-the-mozart-effect-22.

24. Ibid.

Chapter 10: Feature-Length Documentaries

1. A. O. Scott, "Documentaries (In Name Only) of Every Stripe," *New York Times,* October 13, 2010, http://www.nytimes.com/2010/10/17/movies/17scott.html.

2. In journalism, the term *muckraking* describes journalists who dig deep into the "muck" to expose corruption, inequality, greed, and human rights violations. The term dates back to the 1880s when newspaper reporter Nellie Bly pretended to be insane to expose neglectful and brutal care of women at the Women's Lunatic Asylum on Blackwell's Island in New York. Bly's report, "Ten Days in the Madhouse," sparked investigations and changes in the treatment of mentally ill women.

3. C. A. Wolski, "Skewering a Sacred Cow," BoxOfficeMojo, no date, http://www.boxofficemojo.com/reviews/?id=1341&p=.htm.

4. Scott.

5. Josh Modell, "Michael Moore Teases New Movie with Publicity Stunt," A.V. Club, June 13, 2009, http://www.avclub.com/article/michael-moore-teases-new-movie-with-publicity-stun-29180.

6. After the report aired on *PrimeTimeLive*, Food Lion sued ABC for the coverage. Interestingly, the lawsuit did not sue the network for libel (defamation through a false report). The truth of ABC's report was not questioned. Instead, the lawsuit hinged on the reporters' fraudulent employment forms. Dale and Barnett had lied to get jobs at the supermarket. The case was argued and appealed in court. In one ruling, a jury fined the reporters $1 each for their fraudulent applications. In the end, the supermarket chain received $315,000 from ABC.

7. Michael Dobbs, "Pinocchio Time for Al Gore," *Washington Post,* October 25, 2007, http://blog.washingtonpost.com/fact-checker/2007/10/pinocchio_time_for_al_gore_1.html.

8. Dobbs.

9. Newspaper editor Moore was recruited to work as the editor of a national magazine and moved to San Francisco for the job. The editorial position didn't work out. Moore sued the publication and used some of the settlement money to kick-start *Roger & Me.*

10. Jim Rutenberg, "Disney Is Blocking Distribution of Film That Criticizes Bush," *New York Times,* May 5, 2004, http://www.nytimes.com/2004/05/05/us/disney-is-blocking-distribution-of-film-that-criticizes-bush.html.

11. "Fahrenheit 9/11 (2004)," Box Office Mojo, http://boxofficemojo.com/movies/?id=fahrenheit911.htm.

12. "U.S. Labor Law for Farmworkers," Farmworker Justice, 2012, http://farmworkerjustice.org/advocacy-and-programs/us-labor-law-farmworkers.

13. Byron Pitts, "*Harvest of Shame* 50 Years Later," CBS News, November 25, 2010, http://www.cbsnews.com/8301-18563_162-7087361.html.

Chapter 11: Animation

1. James Clarke, *Animated Films* (London: Virgin, 2004), 2.

2. Jennifer L. McMahon, "The Function of Fiction: The Heuristic Value of Homer," in *The Simpsons & Philosophy,* ed. William Irwin, Mark T. Conard, and Aeon J. Skoble (Chicago: Open Court, 2001), 230.

3. Douglas R. Bruce, "Notes Towards a Rhetoric of Animation: The Road Runner as Cultural Critique," *Critical Studies in Media Communication* 18, no. 2 (June 2001): 230.

4. Douglas Rushkoff, *Media Virus* (New York: Ballantine Books, 1996), 109.

5. Quoted in ibid., 109.

6. In New York, printed cartoon strips were popular features in newspapers owned by William Randolph Hearst and Joseph Pulitzer. The first well-known cartoon strip, "Yellow Kid," by Richard Outcault, appeared in Pulitzer's *New York World* in 1895, but competitor Hearst convinced Outcault to defect and draw the cartoon for Hearst's *New York Journal.* Outcault's character and down-to-earth subject matter proved a hit with the working classes who read the newspapers. The character's skin was yellow—and thus the cartoon contributed to the nickname "yellow journalism." The appellation first described newspapers of Hearst and Pulitzer but came to be synonymous with any sensational popular news media.

7. *The Simpson's Movie* trailer, Vimeo, no date, https://vimeo.com/54047894.

8. "*Simpsons Movie* Creators Talk Pig Farms, Pixar, Green Day with Kurt Loder," MTV.com, July 26, 2007, http://www.mtv.com/news/articles/1565599/simpsons-movie-creators-talk-pig-farms-pixar-green-day-with-kurt-loder.jhtml.

9. McMahon.

10. McMahon, 228.

11. Jessica Tholmer, "Everything I Need to Know, I Learned from the Simpsons," Hello Giggles, March 9, 2012. http://hellogiggles.com/everything-i-need-to-know-i-learned-from-the-simpsons.

12. "Animated Soviet Propaganda: American Imperialist, Black and White," directed by I. Ivanov-Vano and L. Amalrik, 1933, YouTube.com, July 4, 2009, http://www.youtube.com/watch?v=P7qiVMgom8g.

13. "Make Mine Freedom," 1948, YouTube.com, June 27, 2006, http://www.youtube.com/watch?v=g_DaMKUP3Og.

14. "Walt Disney Goes to War," *Life,* August 31, 1942, 61, http://books.google.com/books?id=iU4EAAAAMBAJ&lpg=PP1&dq=Walt%20Disney%20Goes%20to%20War%20Life%20magazine%201942&pg=PP1#v=onepage&q&f=false.

15. "The New Spirit," Walt Disney Studios, 943, Internet Archive, https://archive.org/details/TheNewSpirit.

16. "Der Fuehrer's Face," Walt Disney Studios, 1943, Internet Archive, https://archive.org/details/DerFuehrersFace.

17. Marc Eliot, *Walt Disney: Hollywood's Dark Prince* (New York: Harper, 1993), 179.

18. Worldwide box office returns for *Marvel's The Avengers* were $1.5 billion, according to Box Office Mojo. The movies that beat the Buena Vista blockbuster were *Avatar* ($2.8 billion) and *Titanic* ($2.2 billion), both directed by James Cameron. More info at http://boxofficemojo.com/alltime/world/.

19. "Puppies Galore," *Dora The Explorer,* Nick Jr., no date, http://www.nickjr.com/kids-videos/kids-dora-the-explorer-videos.html.

20. Jim Korkis, "Donald Duck Pays His Taxes," Cartoon Institute: Animation World Network, 1999, http://www.awn.com/tooninstitute/toonnews/korkus.htm.

21. Quoted in Rushkoff, 122.

22. "Changing Attitudes on Gay Marriage," Religion and Public Life Project, Pew Research Center, June 2013, http://features.pewforum.org/same-sex-marriage-attitudes/slide2.php.

23. McMahon, 228.

Chapter 12: Sports Media

1. Dave Zirin, *A People's History of Sports in the United States: 250 Years of Politics, Protest, People, and Play* (New York: New Press, 2008), xii.

2. Peter Keating, "NFL Nation," *ESPN Magazine* 5, no. 3, ESPN. go.com, http://espn.go.com/magazine/vol5no03nation.html.

3. Zirin, 268.

4. Ibid., 2–3.

5. John Betts, "Sporting Journalism in Nineteenth-Century America," *American Quarterly* 5, no. 1 (1953): 54.

6. Robert Kolker, *Media Studies: An Introduction* (West Sussex, UK: Wiley & Blackwell, 2009), 147.

7. Roone Arledge and Gilbert Rogin, "It's Sports, It's Money . . . It's TV," *Sports Illustrated,* April 25, 1966, http://sportsillustrated.cnn.com/vault/article/magazine/MAG1078465/1/index.htm.

8. Steven D. Stark, *Glued to the Set: The 60 Television Shows and Events That Made Us Who We Are Today* (New York: Delta, 1997), 49, 210.

9. Andy Benoit, "Football, Baseball, and the Evolving Tastes of Fans," The Fifth Down: NewYork Times NFL blog, *New York Times,* April 17, 2012, http://fifthdown.blogs.nytimes.com/2012/04/17/football-baseball-and-the-evolving-tastes-of-fans/.

10. Jeff MacGregor, "The Day after Yesterday," ESPN.com, February 4, 2013, http://espn.go.com/nfl/playoffs/2012/story/_/id/8913733/the-super-bowl-overtaken-american-culture.

11. Arledge and Rogin.

12. Bryan E. Denham, "Intermedia Attribute Agenda Setting in *The New York Times*: The Case of Animal Abuse in U.S. Horse Racing," *Journalism & Mass Communication Quarterly* 9, no 1 (Spring 2014): 17–37.

13. Mark Fainaru-Wada, interview, August 28, 2006, *PBS Frontline: News Wars,* http://www.pbs.org/wgbh/pages/frontline/newswar/interviews/fainaru-wada.html#3.

14. Ibid.

15. Steve Fainaru, and John Barr, "New Questions about NFL Doctor," ESPN.com, August 18, 2013, http://espn.go.com/ espn/otl/story/_/id/9561661/central-figure-nfl-concussion-crisis-appointed-years-ago-league-position-commissioner -paul-tagliabue-patient.

16. Ibid.

17. Duff Wilson, "Medical Adviser for Baseball Lists Exaggerated Credentials," *New York Times*, March 30, 2005, http://www.nytimes.com/2005/03/30/sports/baseball/30doctor.html.

18. Ibid.

19. Dave Zirin, "ESPN Journalists Speak Out on Concussion Documentary," *The Nation* blog, August 26, 2013, http://www.thenation.com/blog/175895/ espn-journalists-speak-out-concussion-documentary.

20. "Games," August 23, 2011, web podcast, Radiolab.org, http://www.radiolab.org/story/153799-games/.

21. "From the School Games to Rio 2016: 1,000 Days Until a Dream Comes True," Rio2016.com, November 9, 2013, http:// rio2016.com/en/news/news/from-the-school-games-to-rio-2016-1000-days-until-a-dream-comes-true.

22. "The Benefits of Sports Aren't Just Physical," Be Active Your Way blog, Health.gov, May 20, 2012, http://www.health.gov/ paguidelines/blog/post/The-Benefits-of-Playing-Sports-Arent-Just-Physical!.aspx.

23. "Coubertin's Fencing Mask," The Olympic Museum, http:// www.olympic.org/content/museum/mosaic/sport-equipment/ pierre-de-coubertin/.

24. Michele Acuto, "World Politics by Other Means? London, City Diplomacy and the Olympics," *Hague Journal of Diplomacy* 8, no. 4 (2013): 287–311.

25. Kathy Lally, "Outside the Olympics, Pressure on Gay Russians Grows," *Washington Post*, February 16, 2014, http://www. washingtonpost.com/world/olympics/outside-the-olympics-pressure-on-gay-russians-grows/2014/02/16/288a944c-90e7-11e3-b227-12a45d109e03_story.html.

26. Ibid.

27. "Q&A: Media Coverage of Women's Sports," The Women's Sports Foundation, no date, http://www.womenssportsfoundation.org/en/home/advocate/q-and-a-media-coverage-of-womens-sports.

28. Ibid.

29. Andrew C. Billings, James R. Angelini, Paul J. MacArthur, Kimberly Bissell, and Lauren R. Smith, "(Re)Calling London: The Gender Frame Agenda Within NBC's Primetime Broadcast of the 2012 Olympiad," *Journalism and Mass Communication Quarterly* 9, no. 1 (2014): 38–58.

30. Ibid., 49.

31. Ibid., 39.

Chapter 13: Hoaxes, Jokes, and Viruses

1. Jeff Catone, "Top 15 Internet Hoaxes of All Time," Mashable.com, July 15, 2009, http://mashable.com/2009/07/15/internet-hoaxes/.

2. "Spike Lee Settles with Couple after Retweet Blunder," CBS News.com, March 30, 2012, http://www.cbsnews.com/8301-31749_162-57407018-10391698/spike-lee-settles-with-couple-after-retweet-blunder/.

3. "About Scams," Craigslist.org, June 1, 2012, http://www.craigslist.org/about/scams.

4. J. Wolak, D. Finkelhor, K. Mitchell, and M. Ybarra, "Online 'Predators' and Their Victims: Myths, Realities and Implications for Prevention and Treatment," *American Psychologist* 63 (2008): 111–128, http://www.unh.edu/ccrc/pdf/Am%20Psy%202-08.pdf.

5. Ibid.

6. "About Scams."

Appendix B: Media Ownership

1. "Diversity in Media Ownership," Free Press, http://www.free-press.net/diversity-media-ownership.

2. Robert W. McChesney, *Rich Media, Poor Democracy: Communication Politics in Dubious Times* (Chicago: University of Illinois Press, 1999), 3.

3. "Diversity in Media Ownership," Free Press, no date, http://www.freepress.net/diversity-media-ownership.

4. "App Store Sales Top $10 Billion in 2013, Apple.com, press release, January 7, 2014, http://www.apple.com/pr/library/2014/01/07App-Store-Sales-Top-10-Billion-in-2013.html.

5. "Verizon Company Overview. Who Owns The Media?" Free Press, no date, http://www.freepress.net/ownership/chart.

6. "Comcast–Time Warner Cable, MB Docket, 14-57," Federal Communications Commission, no date, http://www.fcc.gov/transaction/comcast-twc.

7. Greg Griffin, "Redstones Settle Feud Over Family Business," *Denver Post*, February 6, 2007, http://www.denverpost.com/search/ci_5164430.